Anonymous

Hand Book to the Parliamentary and Departmental Buildings, Canada

With Plans of the Buildings Indicating the Several Offices....

Anonymous

Hand Book to the Parliamentary and Departmental Buildings, Canada
With Plans of the Buildings Indicating the Several Offices....

ISBN/EAN: 9783337156220

Printed in Europe, USA, Canada, Australia, Japan

Cover: Foto ©Suzi / pixelio.de

More available books at **www.hansebooks.com**

Hand Book

TO THE

PARLIAMENTARY AND DEPARTMENTAL BUILDINGS,

CANADA,

WITH PLANS OF THE BUILDINGS INDICATING THE SEVERAL OFFICES AND THE NAMES OF THE OFFICIALS OCCUPYING THEM ;

TOGETHER WITH A

Plan of the City,

AND A

SHORT SKETCH OF THE VALLEY OF THE OTTAWA AND EVERY OBJECT OF INTEREST IN THE NEIGHBOURHOOD ;

— ALSO —

Lists of Members of the Privy Council,—Local Governments,—Senators,—
Members of the House of Commons and Local Legislatures,
&c., &c., &c.

Price :---25 Cents.

OTTAWA:
PRINTED BY G. E. DESBARATS.

1867.

NOTICE.

THE Compiler of the "HAND BOOK" begs to return his best thanks to those who have assisted him with plans, information, &c., for this little work—the plans were obtained by the Leggo-type process, an invention which, when better known, will prove of great benefit to the publishers and authors, and to which the public are indebted for the low price at which this Book is offered to them.

It is hoped that Lawyers, Land Agents and business men generally, and strangers to Ottawa having transactions with the Government Departments, as well as tourists attracted to Ottawa by the desire of examining one of the noblest pile of buildings yet erected on the Continent of America, will find their way greatly smoothed by the "Hand Book."

TABLE OF CONTENTS.

PLANS.

INDEX TO QUEBEC ADVERTISERS.

INDEX TO OTTAWA ADVERTISERS.

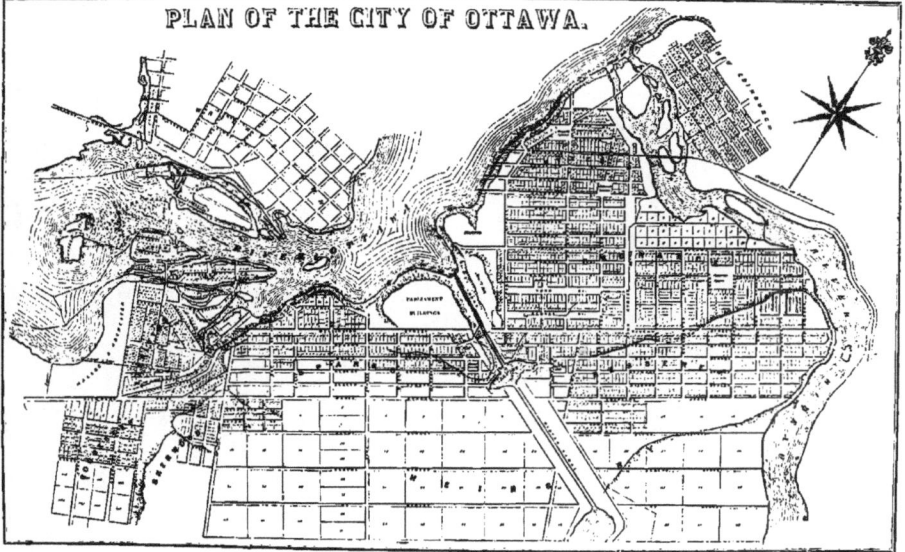

PLAN OF THE CITY OF OTTAWA.

THE QUEEN AND ROYAL FAMILY.

THE QUEEN.—Victoria, of the United Kingdom of Great Britain and Ireland, Queen, Defender of the Faith. Her Majesty was born at Kensington Palace, of May 24, 1819; succeeded to the throne June 20, 1837, on the death of her uncle, King William IV.; was crowned June 28, 1838; and married February 10, 1840, to his Royal Highness Prince Albert. Her Majesty is the only child of his late Royal Highness Edward Duke of Kent, son of King George III. The Children of Her Majesty are :

Her Royal Highness Victoria-Adelaide-Mary-Louisa, PRINCESS ROYAL of ENG-LAND and PRUSSIA, born November 21, 1840; and married to His Royal Highness William of Prussia, January 25, 1858, and has issue two sons and a daughter.

His Royal Highness Albert-Edward, PRINCE of WALES, born November 9, 1841; married March 10, 1863, Alexandra of Denmark (Princess of Wales,) born December 1, 1844; and has issue two sons, Prince Albert-Victor, born January 8, 1864, and George-Frederick-Ernest-Albert, born June 3, 1865.

Her Royal Highness Alice-Maud-Mary, born April 25, 1843 ; Married to His Royal Highness Prince Frederick-Louis of Hesse July 1st, 1862, and has issue two daughters and a son.

His Royal Highness Alfred-Ernest-Albert, born 6th August, 1844.

Her Royal Highness Helena-Augusta-Victoria, born May 25, 1846 ; married to his Royal Highness Prince Frederick-Christian-Charles-Augustus of Schleswig-Holstein-Sonderburg-Augustenburg, July 5, 1866.

Her Royal Highness Louisa-Caroline-Alberta, born March 18, 1848.

His Royal Highness Arthur-William-Patrick-Albert, born May 1, 1850.

His Royal Highness Leopold-George-Duncan-Albert, born April 7, 1853.

Her Royal Highness Beatrice-Mary-Victoria-Feodore, born April 14, 1857.

George-Frederick-William-Charles, K. G., DUKE of CAMBRIDGE, Cousin to Her Majesty, born March 26, 1819.

Augusta-Wilhelmina-Louisa, DUCHESS of CAMBRIDGE, niece of the Landgrave of Hesse and aunt to Her Majesty, born July 25, 1795 ; married, in 1818, the late Duke of Cambridge.

George-Frederick-Alexander-Charles-Earnest-Augustus, K. G., DUKE of CUM-BERLAND, cousin to Her Majesty, born March, 1819 ; married Princess Frederica of Mecklenburg-Strelitz, and has issue a son and two daughters.

Augusta-Caroline-Charlotte-Elizabeth-Mary-Sophia-Louisa, daughter of the late Duke of Cambridge, and cousin to Her Majesty, born July 19, 1822; married, June 28, 1843, to Frederick, Grand Duke of Mecklenburg-Strelitz, and has a son.

Mary-Adelaide-Wilhelmina-Elizabeth, daughter of the late Duke of Cambridge, and cousin to her Majesty, born November 27, 1833 ; married Prince Teck, June 7, 1866.

1868.

January.

S	M	T	W	T	F	S
...	...	...	1	2	3	4
5	6	7	8	9	10	11
12	13	14	15	16	17	18
19	20	21	22	23	24	25
26	27	28	29	30	31	...
...	...					

February.

S	M	T	W	T	F	S
...	...	...	...	...	..	1
2	3	4	5	6	7	8
9	10	11	12	13	14	15
16	17	18	19	20	21	22
23	24	25	26	27	28	29

March.

S	M	T	W	T	F	S
1	2	3	4	5	6	7
8	9	10	11	12	13	14
15	16	17	18	19	20	21
22	23	24	25	26	27	28
29	30	31	...	...	...	...

April.

S	M	T	W	T	F	S
...	...	...	1	2	3	4
5	6	7	8	9	10	11
12	13	14	15	16	17	18
19	20	21	22	23	24	25
26	27	28	29	30	...	...
...	...	...	...	...	...	...

May.

S	M	T	W	T	F	S
...	...	...	...	...	1	2
3	4	5	6	7	8	9
10	11	12	13	14	15	16
17	18	19	20	21	22	23
24	25	26	27	28	29	30
31	...	...	...	...	...	...

June.

S	M	T	W	T	F	S
...	1	2	3	4	5	6
7	8	9	10	11	12	13
14	15	16	17	18	19	20
21	22	23	24	25	26	27
28	29	30	...	...	...	...

July.

S	M	T	W	T	F	S
...	...	...	1	2	3	4
5	6	7	8	9	10	11
12	13	14	15	16	17	18
19	20	21	22	23	24	25
26	27	28	29	30	31	...
...	...	...	...	...	...	...

August.

S	M	T	W	T	F	S
...	...	...	...	...	...	1
2	3	4	5	6	7	8
9	10	11	12	13	14	15
16	17	18	19	20	21	22
23	24	25	26	27	28	29
30	31	...	...	...	...	...

September.

S	M	T	W	T	F	S
...	...	1	2	3	4	5
6	7	8	9	10	11	12
13	14	15	16	17	18	19
20	21	22	23	24	25	26
27	28	29	30	...	...	...

October.

S	M	T	W	T	F	S
...	...	...	...	1	2	3
4	5	6	7	8	9	10
11	12	13	14	15	16	17
18	19	20	21	22	23	24
25	26	27	28	29	30	31
...	...	...	...	...	...	...

November.

S	M	T	W	T	F	S
1	2	3	4	5	6	7
8	9	10	11	12	13	14
15	16	17	18	19	20	21
22	23	24	25	26	27	28
29	30	...	...	...	...	...

December.

S	M	T	W	T	F	S
...	...	1	2	3	4	5
6	7	8	9	10	11	12
13	14	15	16	17	18	19
20	21	22	23	24	25	26
27	28	29	30	31	...	...

BRIEF DESCRIPTION OF THE CHIEF FEATURES OF OTTAWA CITY.

Though the present "Hand Book" was designed chiefly with the view of furnishing tourists with a detailed description of the Parliament and Departmental Buildings of the Dominion of Canada, the Compiler has thought it as well to offer, at the same time, a brief notice of the principal features of interest, both in the City of Ottawa itself, as well as in the surrounding neighborhood.

No stranger can fail to be struck at a glance with the many natural advantages that the City of Ottawa possesses both of beauty and utility, and a closer acquaintance with the *locale* more than confirms the first impression.

Something seems to have inspired its founders with a prophetic vision of its destiny as the future Capital of the Dominion, for it appears from the first to have been laid out on an immense scale.

Its principal streets are of great width and extend from East to West nearly three miles, and throughout the whole of these, the meaner buildings are being gradually displaced by erections worthy of the large thoroughfares upon which they are situated.

The limits of the City do not at present extend more than half a mile back from the Ottawa River frontage, but its natural and ultimate limits are evidently destined to extend to the Rideau Canal, which together with the Rideau River in the rear, and the Ottawa River in its front, will enclose the City site in a Peninsula, the area of which will be three miles long by three miles broad, affording room for a City population of the largest class. The beautiful new gravel road just finished running from Wellington street to the Rideau Canal which it crosses by a swing Bridge, affords an excellent guage for the future breadth of Ottawa City, north and south. It is called Gloucester Road and runs through the property of W. Powell, Esq., Sheriff of Carleton, and is already being taken up by Merchants, Government Officials and others desiring suburban residences, and is resorted to as a favorite drive. This may be pronounced by some a "Day-Dream" but Ottawa has already realized more wonderful

dreams than this, for it is said that the farm on which the City now
stands was sold 37 years ago for Eighty pounds Currency, and surely
the ratio between that sum and its present value, is as marvellous a
fact as anything we can dream of for Ottawa's future, when the
Ottawa and Huron Canal shall have been completed, and when
Ottawa may boast of being not only the Legislative Capital, but the
chief seat of the Manufactures of the Dominion.

THE SCENERY OF OTTAWA.

Ottawa City lies on the right bank or south shore of the Ottawa
River, and may be said to extend from the Chaudière Falls to Rockcliffe,
a distance of about three miles.   Nothing can be more striking than
the *tableau* presented by this Ottawa River frontage of the City as
viewed from the River or from the low shore of the opposite bank.

The whole length presents a succession of bold promontories or
bluffs, many of them rising perpendicularly 250 feet from the water's
edge, clothed with a perpetual green of bushy cedar and pine, and
separated from each other by small bays.

ROCKCLIFFE.

Ascending the river the first of these promontories which presents
itself is known by the name of Rockcliffe, the property of Dr. Hunter,
its frontage extends about a quarter of a mile, and through its whole
length on the side of the cliff runs a magnificent Terrace or Alley,
sufficiently wide for a Carriage Road, and so thickly shaded throughout by tall pine trees and cedar bushes as to be impervious alike to
the fierce summer sun and the chilly blasts of winter.   The view
obtained here of the opposite shore, wherever an opening can be
found, is perhaps more beautiful (as it is more extensive) than from
any of the other promontories, the eye here embraces not only the
pastoral landscape of grassy slopes and cultivated fields, backed by the
distant mountains of Lower Canada, but a clear view sixteen miles
down the Ottawa River.

THE RIDEAU FALLS.

The next striking object met with is the Rideau River tumbling
perpendicularly into the Ottawa River on either side of a low flat
island making two distinct falls of about 40 feet high.

MAJOR'S HILL—BARRACK HILL AND THE PARLIAMENT BUILDINGS.

Major's Hill and Barrack Hill are the two next promontories,—the first is at present used as a Public Park,—the latter which is the glory of Ottawa is crowned by the magnificent new Parliament Buildings, fully described in another place. In the Bay between these two promontories is situated the entrance to the massive Locks of the Rideau Canal, an expensive Imperial work which intersects the City and joins the Rideau River. The old and respectable firm of Dickenson & Co., run a line of freight and passenger steamers from the City of Ottawa to Kingston through this Canal.

CHAUDIERE FALLS.

These falls (spanned by the suspension bridge which unites the provinces of Ontario and Quebec.) though always interesting, and probably more remarkable in their eccentricity than any other falls in the known world, must be viewed at two different seasons of the year to be properly appreciated.

First.—In the Spring when the Ottawa is receiving the swollen waters of its numerous tributaries and when it is said to be discharging as great a volume of water as Niagara itself : on these occasions the foaming and resistless rush of the turbulent torrent fascinates the observer and chains him in bewilderment to the spot.

Secondly.—In mid Winter when the outer waters of the falls are frozen into the most fantastic forms—in some places assuming the appearance of different kinds of drapery, from the heavy curtain to the most transparent lace veil : in other places looking like the fret-work of some elaborate marble altar screen.

RIDEAU HALL.

Rideau Hall is the residence of His Excellency the Governor General. The house is a substantial stone building without architectural pretensions. A handsome new wing of fine proportions has been recently added, containing a spacious reception room, and a suite of apartments on a suitable scale, and fitted with all the conveniences of an English gentleman's residence. It has been newly furnished throughout partly by Messrs. Jacques & Hay, of Toronto, and partly by Mr. Drum, of Quebec, at an expense of about $26,000.

Both these eminent firms have had an opportunity at Rideau Hall of displaying the beauty and excellence to which the art of Upholstery has attained in Canada, and we venture to affirm that nothing more elegant in side-boards, sofas, chairs, and bed-room suits could have been turned out either in London or Paris.

The house stands in about thirty-five acres of ground well laid out, and is approached through a handsome avenue of well grown trees.

MANUFACTURING PROGRESS.

The Staple Trade of Ottawa, as is well known, is the manufacture of Lumber ; and all the Saw Mills round the Chaudière Falls on both sides of the River, as well as at the Rideau Falls, are in the hands of enterprizing Firms from the United States, who are driving a most extensive business in Sawed Lumber, but the prize for enterprize and progress must be awarded to E. B. Eddy, Esq. This gentleman, it appears, came to Ottawa about eleven years ago, possessing nothing but the ingenuity and indomitable energy so characteristic of his countrymen ; to-day his works at the Village of Hull, (which is, after all, but a suburb of the City of Ottawa,) cover 25 acres of ground— they consist of two large saw mills, running 240 lumber saws, a barrel, pail and match manufactory, all built in the most substantial manner and probably superior in their machinery and improvements to any similar establishment in the world. Eddy's Matches, it appears, have been proved to be the most reliable of any in the market and are not only esteemed in America but are largely imported into Europe. We have no space to describe in detail the economy of this establishment, but the reader may form some idea of the extent of its operations, when we state, that a good sized village population of 1200 people— men, women, and children—are employed by Mr. Eddy's enterprize.

The employment of the Ottawa River Water Power, may, however, be said to be only at its commencement, as the Government intend to stretch a Dam across the River above the Chaudière Falls ; we may therefore, in due time, expect to see Cotton, Woollen and other Manufactures established here.

Among the general improvements finished and progressing in Ottawa and its suburbs we may notice

THE RESIDENCE OF J. M. CURRIER, ESQ.

On the Ottawa River, in front of Rideau Hall, Mr. Currier, the Member of the Commons for the City, has nearly completed a beautiful house on the Bluff next to Rockcliffe. The design is Modern Gothic in Grey Lime Stone with Cut Stone Dressings, the Chimneys, Windows, Doors and other stone finishings are beautifully executed. Its interior is fitted with Water Tank, heating apparatus, Baths, &c., all on the newest principle; in the grounds is a beautiful vinery, the road frontage has a fine Lawn shaded by large Oak and Pine Trees. On the whole this is a perfect Gem of Domestic Architecture. On the extreme edge of the Bluff and commanding a view of similar scenery to that seen from Rockcliffe is an elegant and capacious Double Storied Summer House.

Daly street is supposed to be the West End or 5th Avenue District of Ottawa. The Upper ten of Government Officials have located here and here also several of the Merchants of the City have erected pretty residences.

RIDES AND DRIVES.

In beautiful rides and drives the neighborhood of Ottawa can scarcely be excelled—a nine mile drive up the Gatineau Road and through Chelsea conduct the tourist to the Mountain Range which forms such a conspicuous object in the scenery viewed from the City of Ottawa. In these mountains are to be found several lovely valleys—with cultivated farms; and Lakes teeming with Trout.

CHURCHES AND OTHER BUILDINGS.

Ottawa is somewhat behind in Ecclesiastical Architecture. The population is half Roman Catholic and half Protestant. The former have a handsome Cathedral, and St. Joseph's Church attached to St Joseph's College is a neat structure, more elegant in its interior than in its exterior design. The Revd. Dr. Jones, on Daly Street, and the Revd. J. J. Johnson, both popular preachers of the English Episcopal Church have been enabled by their respective Congregations to erect recently neat little Gothic Churches holding 400 or 500 people each, but from some cause or other there is no English Episcopal Church worthy of the place, nor any present prospect of so desirable an addition to Ottawa's Ecclesiastical Buildings.

Of other erections which have struck us as examples worthy of imitation by their fellow citizens, we may mention the handsome block of Brick Stores on Sussex St., erected by His Lordship the B. C. Bishop of Ottawa,—the Offices of Messrs. Hamilton,—Desbarats Government Printing Office and Block.—The Quebec Bank which besides its handsome exterior has recently received internal deco-

rations of great beauty both of design and execution—the handsome
and commodious New Wing in cut stone added to the Russell Hotel
by D. McLaughlin, Esq., M. P.

And having conducted our visitor thus far we beg to take our
leave of him, but before making our bow we take the liberty of intro-
ducing him to James Gouin, Esq., the cheery polite and attentive host
of the Russell, one of that class of landlords without which no hotel
of whatever pretensions can establish a good reputation, but with
which necessary adjunct the humblest hotel may make the weary
traveller feel at home.

The population of Ottawa is supposed now to have attained to
25,000.

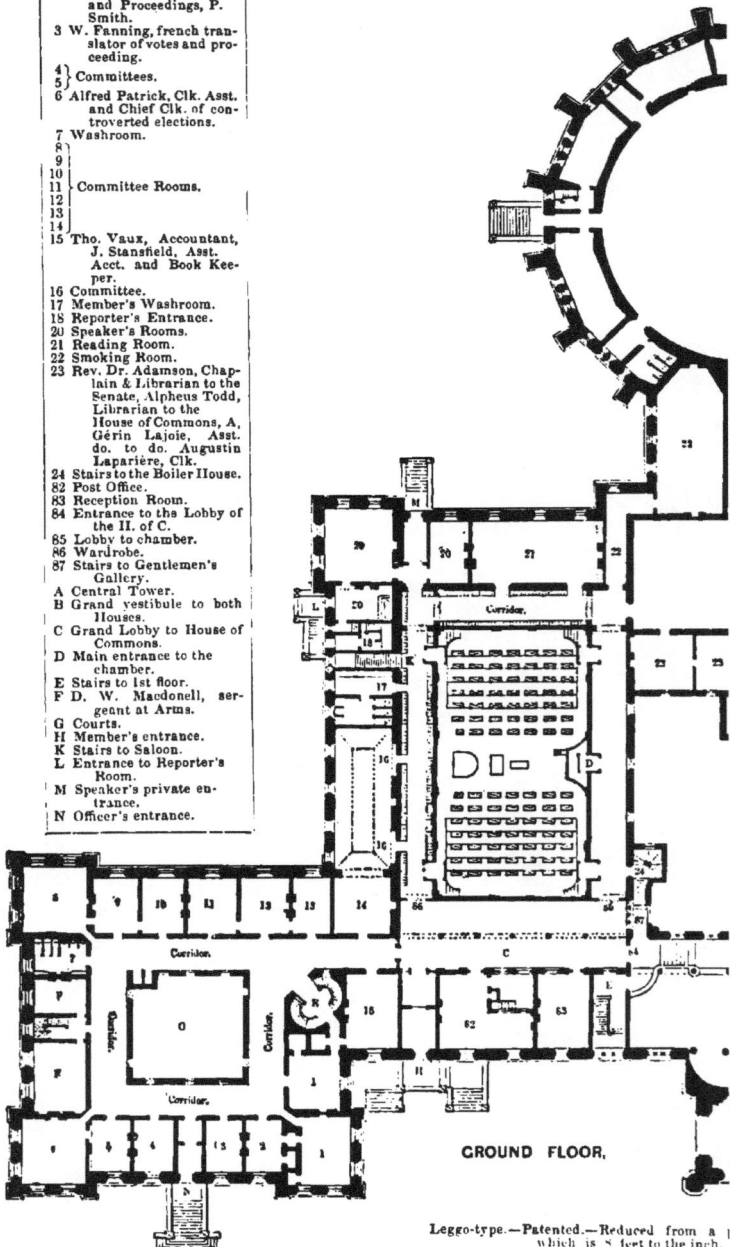

GROUND FLOOR,

Leggo-type.—Patented.—Reduced from a which is 8 feet to the inch.

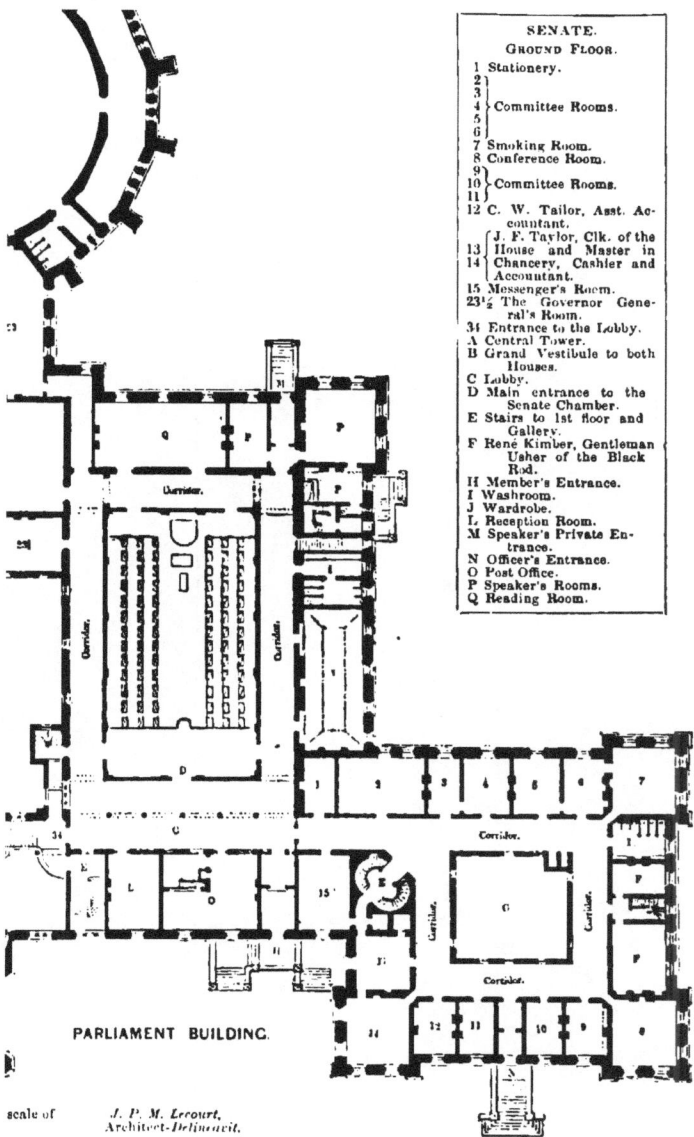

PARLIAMENT BUILDING.

scale of   J. P. M. Lecourt,
                  Architect-Delineavit.

HOUSE OF COMMONS.
1st. Floor.

25 J. E. Dorion, Assistant
French translator, R.
Sulte, extra do A.
Genand do.

26 T. J. Coursolles, Asst.
French translator, J.
F. Gingras, do.

26 E. Blain, French translator, L. McKay do.

28 E. P. Dorion, Asst.
French Law Clk. and
chief French transla-
tor, C. A. Gagnon, Ge-
neral Asst. and proof
reader.

29 F. Badgley, Asst. Law
Clk. chief english
translator, W. Wilson.

30 F. Hayes, W. Wilson, Jr.

31 G. W. Wicksteed, Q. C.,
Law Clerk.

32 Washroom, &c.

33 Assistant Clerk.

34 Lachevrotière & Bowles,
Clerks to Clerk Asst.

35 Pierre Rivet, french journal Clerk, N. F. Bel-
court, W. B. Ross,
english journal Clerk,
A. G. D. Taylor, Asst.
do H. Lindsay, do.

36 H. Hartney, chief office
Clerk, and Clerk to
joint com. on Printing.

37 H. B. Stewart, English
writing Clerk, J. Blais.
E. Dénéchaud, H.
R. Smith, Jr., Clerks.

38 Stationery office, J. S.
Sloane.

39 Stationery.

40 J. P. Leprohon, 1st Clerk
of Committees.

41. F. X. Blanchette. 2nd
Clerk of Commitees.

42 Committee room.

43 G. H. Macaulay, Speaker's
Secretary.

44 F. MacGillivray, Clerk
of Routine and Records.

45 Vestibule to caucus room.

46 Caucus room (tower.)

47 Records of Clk. of the
Crown in Chancery.

48 Ed. J. Langevin, Clk. of
the Crown in Chy.

49 Thaddeus Patrick, Clerk
of Railway Committee.

50 Alfred Todd, chief clerk
of Private Bills, and
Chs. Panet.

53 Door to Senator's Gallery.

54 " to Ladies' "

56 " to Reporters' "

58 Reporter's Room.

60 } Reporter's Washroom.
62 } &c.

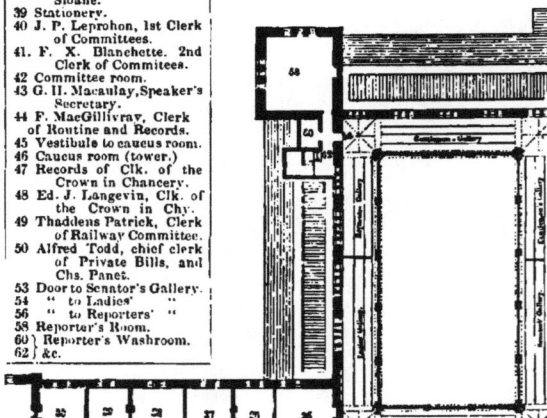

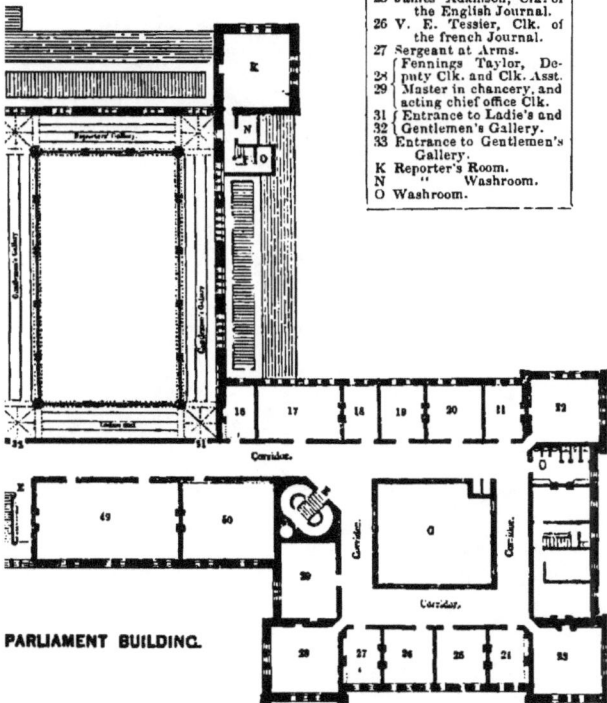

PARLIAMENT BUILDING.

Leggo-type.—Patented.—Reduced from a plan the scale of which is 8 feet to the inch.

THE GOVERNMENT BUILDINGS.

Ottawa having been selected by Her Majesty, as the Capital of Canada, the sum of £75,000 was voted by the Legislative Assembly, for the erection of a Parliament House, and a premium of $1000 offered for the best design not to exceed that amount, Messrs. Fuller & Jones were the successful architects, and although the design was considered by many as too costly, responsible contractors were found who tendered within the government vote. Upon examination, however, of the spot selected for the erection, formerly known as the Barrack Hill, it was found from the inequality of the ground, that immense excavations were necessary, which made in solid rock added enormously to the original cost, and could not have been foreseen by builders nor architects. The government finding no provision for this work in the grant, and fearing it would cost a large portion of the original sum voted, stopped works, and for some considerable time there was no progress. A commission of inquiry was appointed, fresh contracts were signed, and the whole of the works placed under the superintendence of Mr. Fuller, under whose management the present highly creditable structures have been completed. The corner stone was laid with great ceremony by His Royal Highness the Prince of Wales, in September, 1860, on which occasion the rejoicings partook of the nature of the place, the lumber arches and men being a novelty to most of its visitors, bullocks and sheep were roasted whole upon the government ground and all comers were feasted. The site of these buildings has been very happily selected in the most elevated part of the city; they consist of the Parliament and two Departmental Buildings, forming three sides of a large square, facing the city, and from their position overlooking most of the houses. In the rear of the Parliament Building the rock descends almost perpendicularly to the river Ottawa; from here the view is truly magnificent, and cannot be surpassed on this continent nor in Europe. The broad river is in itself a beautiful object, but the vast extent of distant forest and hill completely absorbs every attention. From this point the Chaudière Falls are distinctly seen, and by some considered more romantic than those of Niagara ; beyond can be traced the island-dotted rapids of the Upper Ottawa. This river must be always interesting on account of its slides, booms, and distinctive race of lumbermen ; it is only seen however to its full advantage in the spring of the year, with high water, crowded with rafts. The group of buildings form a most picturesque object from every approach to the city, and can be seen at a great distance.

The Parliament Buildings stand on a high plateau of some 30 acres in area. The buildings form three sides of a quadrangular figure, and are widely detached. The Parliament or main building facing Wellington street ; and the Departmental Buildings facing inwards to the square and forming the other two sides of the figure. The splendour of these Buildings, their fine commanding site, together with the beauty of the surrounding scenery, place them in a very enviable position—compared with all other structures used for similar purposes on this continent, and some say, even in Europe— and must ever make them objects of interest to the tourist and the stranger.

The style of the Buildings is the Gothic of the 12th and 13th Centuries, with modification to suit the climate of Canada. The ornamental work and the dressing round the windows are of Ohio sandstone. The plain surface is faced with a cream-colored sandstone of the Potsdam formation, obtained from Napean, a few miles from Ottawa. The spandrils of the arches, and the spaces between windowarches and the sills of the upper windows, are filled up with a quaint description of stone-work, composed of stones of irregular size, shape and colour, very neatly set together. These with the Potsdam red sandstone employed in forming the arches over the windows, afford a pleasant variety of colour and effect, and contrast with the general masses of light coloured sandstone, of which the body of the work is composed.

This Building, as you approach from Wellington street, presents a very imposing appearence. The central of the seven towers, which is very rich in design, projects its width from the front of the Building, and when completed, will be about 180 ft. high. The body of the building in front is forty feet high, above which rises the slanting roofs of slate, surmounted by lines of ornamental iron cresting. The building is 472 feet long ; and the depth from the front of the main tower to the rear of the library is 570 feet, covering an area of 82,886 superficial feet. It stands at a distance of 600 feet from Wellington street, so that the quadrangle formed on three sides by the Buildings and on the fourth by the street, is 700 feet from east to west, and 600 feet from north to south ; thus affording a very spacious square.

41

42

43

44

Corridor.

22

21

20

Corridor.

Boiler House

19 18 17 16

Corridor.

D

B

1 2

A

DEPARTMENTAL BUILDI

VIEW FACING 70

CUSTOM'S DEPT.

10 The Hon. the Minister of Customs.
35 R. S. M. Bouchette, Com. of Customs.
9 —Bliss, Secretary.
36 J. W. Peachy, J. C. Audy.
37 J. R. Audy.
24 H. H. Duffil.
25 Waiting Room.
26 P. E. Sheppard, G. M. Mailleue, H. C. Hay.
27 ——————
28 —Johnson.
38 W. A. Bell, J. F. Wolff.
39 Stationery.

INLAND REVENUE DEPT.

29 The Hon. the Minister of Inland Revenue.
31 Thos. Worthington, Dy. do.
32 L. O'Brien, J. F. Brown.
30 ——————
34 Messengers.

RECR. GEN'L'S DEPT.

7 The Hon. the Receiver General.
6 T. D. Harington, Dy. Rer. J. B. H. Neeve.
4 G. C. Reiffenstein, C. W. Shay.
12 T. C. Bramley.
11 J. B. Stanton, L. F. Dufresne.

14 F. Lewis.
5 J. F. Pellant.
15 F. Hunter.
8. Waiting room.
13 Keeper's room.

MINISTER OF FINANCE.

44 The Hon. the Minister of Finance.
21 W. Dickinson, Dy. do.
42 N. Godard, R. W. Baxter.
40 J. Drysdale, P. Ryan.
41 A. Cary, R. J. Killaly.
23 F. Q. Scott.
22 C. J. Anderson, H. A. Jones.
43 W. A. Blackmore, Secretary, J. A. Torrance.
20 Messengers.

AUDITOR'S DEPT.

1 J. Langton, Auditor.
3 J. Simpson, Asst. do.
2 A. Harvey, J. R. Hall.
16 E. C. Barber, J. Patterson.
17 Thos. Cruse, H. Cotton.
18 ——————
19 J. B. Simpson, G. M. Jarvis.
A Entrance.
B Stairs.
C Washroom.
D Tower.

GROUND FLOOR, (EASTERN BLOCK.)

LINGTON STREET, AND COUNTRY SOUTH

Leggo-type.—Patented.—Reduced from a plan the scale of which is 8 feet to the inch.

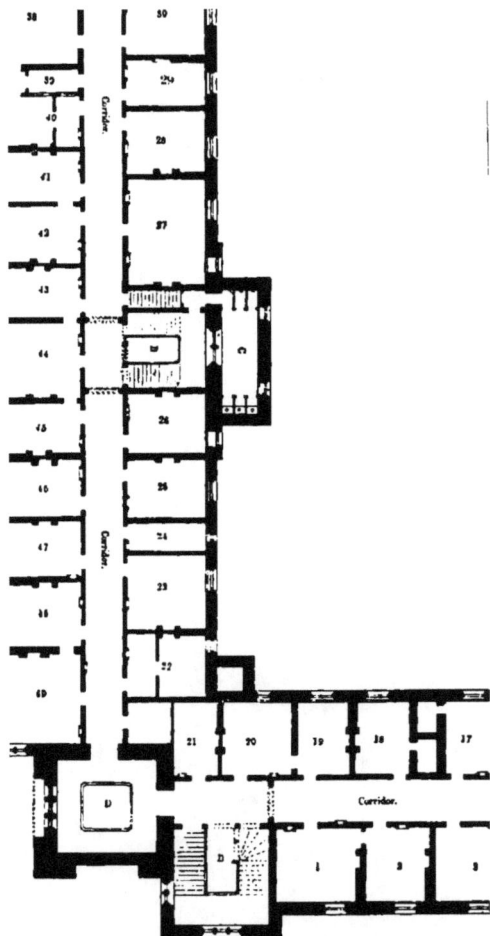

DEPARTMENTAL BUIL.

VIEW FACING TOWARDS

J. P. M. Lecourt,
Architect-Delineavit.

FIRST FLOOR, (EASTERN BLOCK.)

TON STREET, AND COUNTRY SOUTH.

Leggo-type.—Patented.—Reduced from a plan the scale of which is 8 feet to the inch.

The ground upon which the buildings stand varies somewhat in elevation, that forming the site of the Parliament Building being the highest. The basement floor of the buildings is assumed to be 250 feet above the ordinary summer level of the river, while that of the Eastern and Western blocks is 135 and 142 feet respectively. The increased elevation, however, improves very much the general effect of the buildings.

The main entrance is through the principal tower, the spacious arches of which admit of a carriage way under them. The piers which support the tower are ornamented with pillars of polished Arnprior marble. Passing through it we enter a large hall, paved with tiles, and also surrounded with marble pillars. Ascending and moving towards the left we come to the Chamber of Commons. The Room measures 90 by 45 feet, the ceiling being over 60 feet high, and formed of fine open work. The skylights above this intermediate ceiling, with the stained glass windows at the sides, throw a plentiful soft light over the whole place. The room is surrounded by large piers of a light greyish marble from Portage du Fort, surmounted just above the galleries by clusters of small pillars of the dark Arnprior ; the arches supported by these pillars being again of the light coloured marble. The galleries can accommodate about 1,000 persons. The Gallery for the Reporters are situated above the Speaker's chair.

On the right of the Main entrance, is the Senate Chamber, alike in every particular to that of the Commons. Along the Corridors you see numerous Rooms for Committee, Clerks, Reading and Smoking.

Although the Library is not yet completed, we, nevertheless, give here a sketch of what is intended to be done. The library will be situated in the rear of the Parliament Building, and the plan is of a polygon of sixteen sides, 90 feet in diameter ; outside of the main room is an aisle of one story high, which is formed of a series of small retiring rooms, where persons desiring a few hours of uninterrupted study can secure it. A corridor will connect the Library with the main building : this corridor will be the picture gallery, but is at present used for the Library. The floors of this building, as well as those of the Departmental Buildings, are made of concrete, perfectly fire-proof ; an invention not long adopted in Europe.

The Eastern Block of the Departmental Buildings is of an irregular and picturesque shape. The west front or that which faces the square, is 245 feet, and 319 feet on the south front or that which faces Wellington street, and cover an area of 41,840 superficial feet. In this building are found the Governor General's Office, the Privy Council room, the Minister of Justice, the Minister of Militia, the

Secretary of State, the Finance and Audit Offices, the Registrar, the Receiver General, the Secretary of State for the Provinces, the Customs and the Inland Revenue departments.

From the east side of this building an extensive view is obtained, embracing the lower town and the country beyond it. Nearer is a plateau, somewhat similar to that upon which stand the buildings, and known as the Major's Hill, and in a deep hollow between and immediately under the walls, is the long chain of Locks of the Rideau Canal, famous for its workmanship and solidity, spanned, a little higher up, by the Sappers' bridge, connecting the lower town with upper and central towns.

The Western Block is similar in style to that of the Eastern block, but not quite so large and more regular in its contruction, being 220 feet long, facing the square, and 277 feet on the south looking on Wellington street. It is also very imposing, although not possessing such good entrance as the Eastern block, a circumstance which is probably accounted for by the fact of the Governor General and Privy Council's rooms being situated in the first described block. The Public Works Department, the Post Office Department, the Adjutant General and Militia Departments, the Marine and Fisheries Department, the Bureau of Agriculture, and the model room connected with the Patent Department, are all located in this building. The west front of this building looking upon the upper town and beyond it towards the Chaudière Falls, and Hull, gives a fine view of the wooded lands on the shore of the Ottawa River and the distant range of hills beyond, including a far view of the river and its banks stretching to the south-west in the direction of Aylmer. Similar or still more extensive views can be obtained from the west side of the Parliament Building.

The ceiling of the passages and of many of the rooms of the Parliament Buildings are made of pine wood, varnished, which being wrought into ornamental cornices and panels produce a rich and very fine appearance. The same material has been used for the doors. The fillings around the grates and mantle-pieces are of polished Arnprior marble; it is greyish blue marble of very fine grain, and capable of being polished to a high degree. All the floors are supported by rolled iron girders, and filled in between with cement. The stairs in the buildings are all built of blue Ohio stone, and constructed with hanging steps.

The system for heating and ventilating is on the most approved principle. Under the central court of the Parliament building is the boiler room, in which are six boilers, each twenty feet long and five feet in diameter, furnished with a steam-drum, safety-valve, &c., and

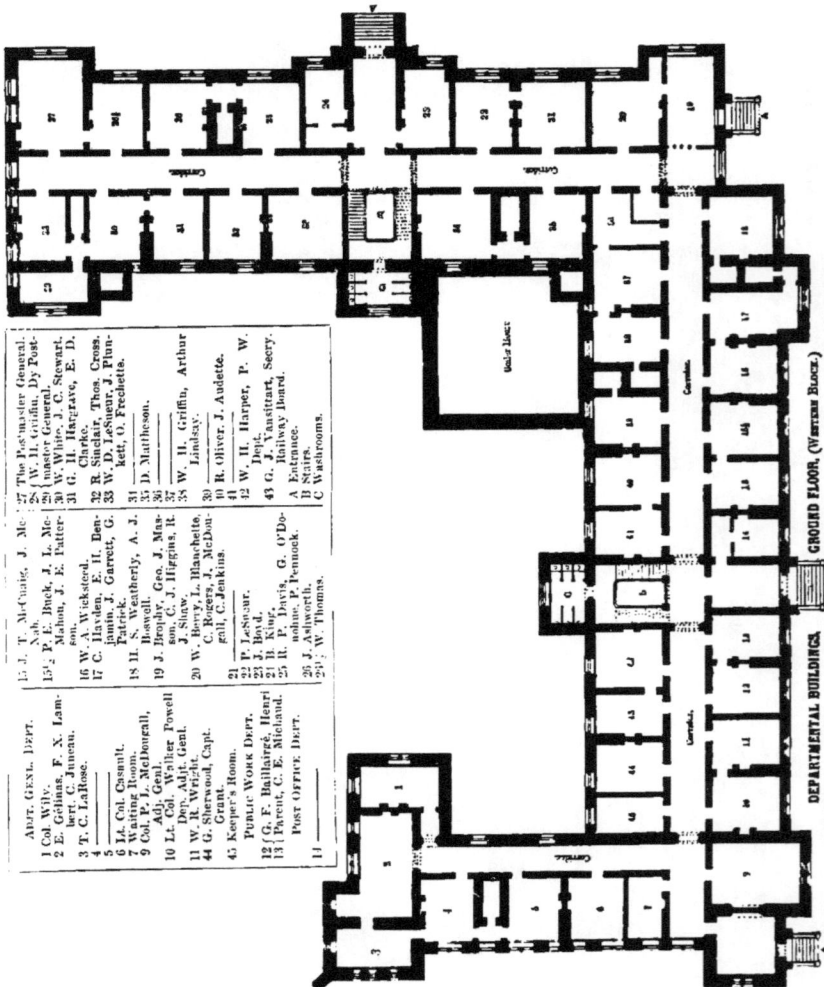

DEPARTMENTAL BUILDINGS. GROUND FLOOR, (WESTERN BLOCK.)

VIEW FACING TOWARDS WELLINGTON STREET, AND COURTNY NORTH.

J. P. M. Lecourt,
Architect.—Delineavit.

Lergo-tyne.—Patented.—Reduced from a plan the scale of which is 8 feet to the inch.

ADJT. GENL. DEPT.
1 Col. Wily.
2 E. Gélinas, F. X. Lambert, C. Juneau.
3 T. C. LaRose.
4
6 Lt. Col. Casault.
7 Waiting Room.
9 Col. P. L. McDonnall, Adj. Genl.
10 Lt. Col. Walker Powell Den. Adjt. Genl.
11 W. R. Wright.
44 G. Sherwood, Capt. Grant.
45 Keeper's Room.

PUBLIC WORK DEPT.
12 { G. F. Baillairgé, Henri
13 { Parent, C. E. Mieland.

POST OFFICE DEPT.
11

15 J. T. McQuaie, J. McNah.
15½ P. E. Buck, J. L. McMahon, J. E. Patterson.
16 W. A. Wicksteed.
17 C. Hayden, E. H. Benjamin, J. Garrett, G. Patrick.
18 H. S. Weatherly, A. J. Boswell.
19 J. Brojdy, Geo. J. Manson, C. J. Higgins, R. J. Shaw.
20 W. Berry, L. Blauchette, C. Rogers, J. McDougall, C. Jenkins.
21 P. LeSueur.
22 J. Boyd.
23 B. King.
25 R. P. Davis, G. O'Donohue. P. Pennock.
26 J. Ashworth.
29½ W. Thomas.

27 The Postmaster General.
28 W. H. Griffin, Dy Postmaster General.
30 W. White, J. C. Stewart.
31 G. H. Hargrave, E. D. Clarke.
32 R. Sinclair, Thos. Cross.
33 W. D. LeSueur, J. Plunkett, O. Frechette.
31 D. Matheson.
35 D. Matheson.
36
38 W. H. Griffin, Arthur Lindsay.
39 R. Oliver, J. Audette.
41
42 W. H. Harper, P. W. Dept.
43 G. J. Vansittart, Seery. Railway Board.
A Entrance.
B Stairs.
C Washrooms.

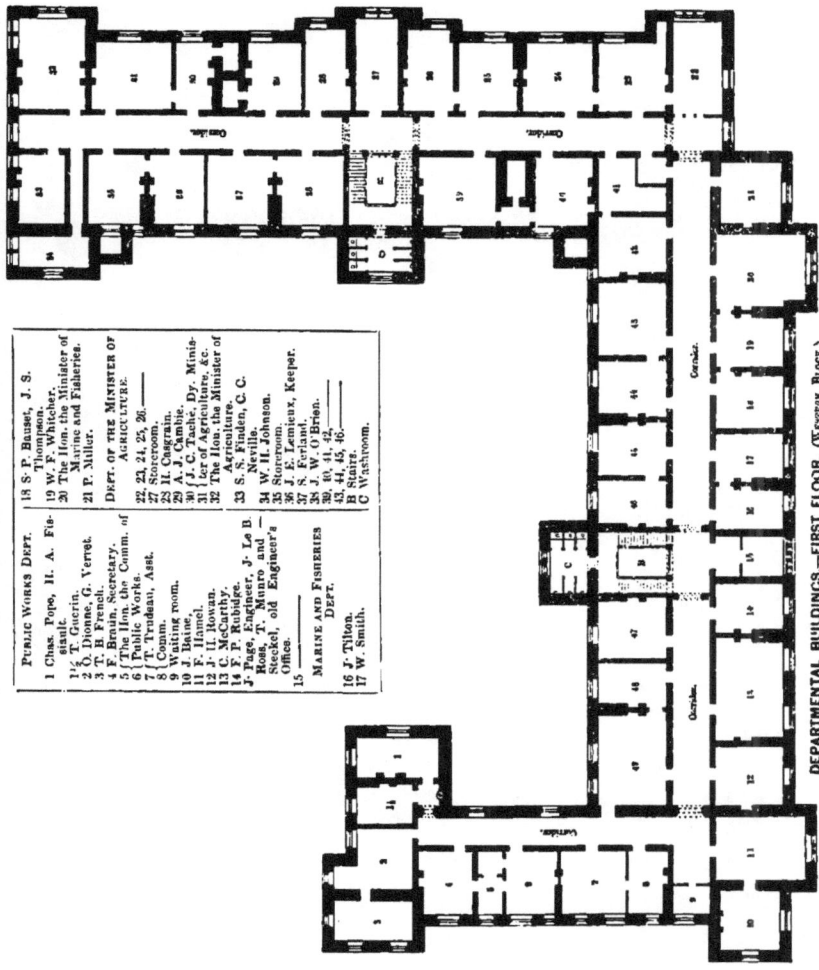

PUBLIC WORKS DEPT.

1 Chas. Pope, H. A. Fisault.
1½ T. Guerin.
2 O. Dionne, G. Verret.
3 T. B French.
4 F. Braun, Secretary.
5 {The Hon. the Comm. of Public Works.
6 {T. Trudeau, Asst.
7 {Comm.
8 {Comm.
9 Waiting room.
10 J Baine.
11 F. Hamel.
12 J. H. Howan.
13 C. McCarthy.
14 F. P. Rubidge.
J. Page, Engineer, J. Le B. Ross, T. Munro and Steckel, old Engineer's Office.
15

MARINE AND FISHERIES DEPT.

16 J. Tilton.
17 W. Smith.

18 S. P. Bausel, J. S. Thompson.
19 W. F. Whitcher.
20 The Hon. the Minister of Marine and Fisheries.
21 P. Mitler.

DEPT. OF THE MINISTER OF AGRICULTURE.

22, 23, 24, 25, 26.
27 Storeroom.
28 H. Chagrain.
29 A. J. Cambie.
30 {J. C. Taché, Dy. Minister of Agriculture, &c.
31 {er of Agriculture, &c.
32 The Hon. the Minister of Agriculture.
33 S. Finden, C. C. Neville.
34 W. H. Johnson.
35 Storeroom.
36 J. E. Lemieux, Keeper.
37 S. Ferland.
38 J. W. O'Brien.
39, 40, 41, 42,
43, 44, 45, 46.
B Stairs.
C Washroom.

DEPARTMENTAL BUILDINGS.—FIRST FLOOR. (WESTERN BLOCK.)

VIEW FACING TOWARD WELLINGTON STREET, AND COUNTRY SIDE

Leggo-type.—Patented.—Reduced from a plan the scale of which is 3 feet to the inch.

J. P. M. Lecourt,
Architect-Delineavit.

a steam engine of sufficient horse power to work the pumps and throw 250 gallons of water per minute into tanks placed in the towers, from whence the water is supplied to all parts of the buildings. The heating is effected by steam conveyed in pipes from these boilers to the Senate Chamber, the Library, and the rooms adjoining, by means of a duct sufficiently large for the introduction of an abundant supply of fresh air, situated immediately under a vault in which steam pipes are placed to warm the air on its entering the vault from the duct, through a perforated floor, and before it passes into rooms proposed to be heated. These ducts enter on all sides of the building, and range in size according to the position in which they are placed. Of the ducts, there are 3,600 lineal feet, generally of 2 feet 4 inches high, with sides built of dressed stone and formed with slight descent where they pass out of the building. The other parts of the building are heated on what is called the coil system, or by direct radiation. For the rooms heated by this system there is an area of 4,308 feet of hot air flues, 24 by 19 inches sectional area, formed in the wall adjoining the committee rooms and other parts of the building heated, exclusive of ninety feet of others of greater dimensions for the larger steam pipes.

In the internal arrangement nothing appears to have been spared to make the buildings as perfect as possible. The wants of the government and its officials have been most carefully studied by the architects, and when all is completed, the beauty of the situation, combined with the elegance of the buildings, will enable the capitol of Canada to compare with any in the world.

Messieurs Fuller and Jones were the Architects, and Mr. Thomas McGreevey, the Contractor for the Parliament Building.

Messieurs Stent and Laver, the Architects, and Messieurs Jones, Haycock & Co., the contractors for the Departmental Buildings. Mr. Charles Garth is the person who successfully carried out the system for heating and ventilation.

THE OTTAWA RIVER.

" .... The Ottawa Country is
" little known, but no man visits its magnificent
" scenery, no man begins to understand its enor-
" mous resources, without an expression of admira-
" tion at the one and surprise at the other."..............

That portion of the Country which is drained by the River Ottawa, and its tributaries, is very little known by the majority of the
Canadian people, except those who are immediately connected with
the lumber business. The great valley of the Ottawa lies in the very
center of Canada ; the river itself dividing the Provinces of Ontario
and Quebec, and including nearly one-fourth of its whole territorial
extent. This valley contains an area of about 80,000 square miles,
and furnishes one of the most valuable portions of our Exports.

The River Ottawa, is supposed to take its source in about 49o of
North Latitude, and 76o of West Longitude. The river winds its
course through the forest solitudes, known only to hunters and
the scattered agents of the Hudson Company, which lie on the
slope of the highlands that separate its waters from those of Hudson's
Bay. On its course it receives many tributaries, and expands into
large lakes. At about 300 miles from its supposed source, and 440
from its mouth at Bout de l'Isle, below Montreal, the Ottawa takes
the Indian name of Lake Temiscaming, which turns at right angles
nearly to its former course and extends for 67 miles unbroken by fall
or rapid. At the head of this lake the Ottawa receives its tributary
called La Blanche ; this streams runs north, for about 90 miles.
Near the outlet of the Blanche; to the west, is the Keetacummaw, a
stream of about 50 miles in length.

The next tributary, on the Ontario side is the Montreal River,—
its mouth being 34 miles below that of the Blanche ; its course is
120 miles north-west, and communicates with Lake Temangamingue ;
this Lake communicates with Lake Nipissing by Sturgeon River.
Between Lake Nipissing, the River Montreal and the River Ottawa,
the whole country is intersected by lakes of various sizes, all com-
municating together.

The Keepawa-sippi tributary, 6 miles lower down, on the opposite side, is the mysterious river of Canada. It proceeds from a lake known as Keepawa. It is said that at a short distance from its mouth, there is a series of Cascades, 120 feet in height, but at a distance of a half mile from its mouth nothing is seen of a cataract, nor can we hear the sound of such a body of water falling. This river and the lake from which it proceeds, are connected with a chain of smaller lakes, from one of which proceeds the River du Moine, which empties itself into the Ottawa, some 100 miles lower down.

The Long Sault Rapid, at the outlet of Lake Temiscaming, is 6 miles in length, and succeeded by another expansion of the Ottawa called the Seven League Lake, into which the Antony empties itself, on the south side ; and is succeeded by the Rapid Les Montagnes, and that at a short distance by another dangerous rapid called Les Erables ; at the foot of this rapid on the north side, the River Nattawissi discharges itself with a fall of 50 feet, and a volume of water equal to that of the Montmorency Fall, near Quebec.

The cave or cellar is the next Rapid ; then comes the Matawan, just above the mouth of the River of the same name. This river runs, in a westerly direction, and is separated from Lake Nipissing by a short portage only ; this is the route taken by the officers and voyageurs of the Hudson's Bay Company in going to the far west, and is the shortest and most direct way from the Province of Quebec and the Eastern States to Lake Superior and the Pacific Ocean. This river, Lake Nipissing, and French River directly connect the Ottawa with Lake Huron, and in this direction, eventually, will pass, by Railroad or Canal, the whole traffic between the seaboard of the North-western States and the Great Lakes, and finally to the Pacific.

The Levielle is followed by the Trou, at the head of which, on the North, is the mouth of the Magna-sippi, a small stream, and the Rapid Deux Rivières, which has three distinct falls. This rapid is succeeded by the great falls known as the Rocher Capitaine ; in which also there is three falls ; the central fall in its wild and picturesque grandeur, its great extent, the rugged masses of rock by which the water is broken, and the great velocity of its dark and deep current, presents one of the most magnificent views on the river.

On the north side, below the Rocher Capitaine, is the mouth of Bear River, and three miles below that, on the same side, the mouth of the Du Moine ; on the south side is the mouth of Grant Greek, and then we have the Rapid Deux Joachim. This is a tremendous rapid, through which no cribs can pass without being smashed to pieces ; in order to avoid this rapid, the government constructed slides and dams at a great expense.

At this point, there is a good hotel, and it may be called the verge of civilisation, for at this place is the last post office. Between Pembroke and the Deux Joachim a steamer plys three times a week. No one who is any way particular about his own comfort should attempt to go further; the progress can be accomplished by canoe, and the numerous rapids, compelling frequent portages, make further travel upward a work of some labour, but for those who are fond of adventures and excitement, nothing could be more desirable. From the point on which is the Hotel, the view is one of the finest in the Country ; the river runs in a straight direction for 43 miles, south-east, bounded on the north side by a high mountain chain, partially wooded, and on the south by a richly wooded and gradually ascending range of hills, resembling the " palisades " on the Hudson River.

From the entrance of the Ottawa into Lake Temiscaming, to the end of the expansion, is 67 miles ; the Long Sault Rapid 6 miles ; Seven League Lake is 17 miles, thence to the Mattawan 13 miles, and the succession of navigable reaches and Rapids to the Deux Joachim 50 miles ; the total distance from the foot of Lake Temiscaming to the City of Ottawa being about 263 miles by the course of the river.

From the foot of the Deux Joachim Rapids to the foot of Upper Allumette Lake ; (another expansion of the Ottawa River,) two miles below the village of Pembroke, is an uninterrupted reach of deep and navigable water. The upper part of it called Deek River is bounded by mountains on the north side, a thousand feet high, while the Allumette Lake is studied with innumerable beautifully wooded Islands, the whole scene far surpassing in grandeur the celebrated Thousand Islands on the River St. Lawrence.

Passing the short Rapid of the Allumette, and turning northward round the lower end of the Allumette Island, fourteen miles long, and eight wide, we enter Lake Coulonge, another expansion of the Ottawa, at the end of which the channel is again divided by the Calumet Island, in all a reach of navigable water for 50 miles. The mountains which border Lake Coulonge on the north rises to about 1,500 feet, and present a beautiful and varied scenery.

On the Upper Allumette Lake, on the Ontario side, is the mouth of the Petawawee, one of the largest and most important tributaries of the Ottawa, being amply provided with the finest timber, is 140 miles in length, and drains an area of 2,200 square miles ; 9 miles below this, on the same side, is the mouth of a small stream called Indian River. Upon it is situated the thriving and busy little town of Pembroke, the capital of the Upper Ottawa.

At the head of Lake Coulonge on the north side, is the mouth of the Black River, 130 miles in length, and draining an area of 1,120 square miles ; and on the same side, 9 miles lower down, is the mouth of the Coulonge, 160 miles long, draining an area of 1,800 square miles. The finest pine timber is produced on both these rivers.

From the head of the Calumet Falls to the Village of Portage du Fort, the Rapids are impassable, and the scenery the grandest imaginable. The timber is taken past these Rapids by means of slides, constructed at great expense by Government. The Rapids on the south side of the Calumet Islands are called the Rocher Fendu ; the principal rapids on the north side are the Grand Calumet, the Derangès and the Sables.

Here we have come to a pretty and flourishing village called Portage du Fort ; there is a macadamised road to the head of the Calumet Rapids, from which point a steamer runs to Pembroke, a distance of thirty miles. Opposite Portage du Fort there is an excellent waggon road, which brings to a small steamer plying on Muskrat Lake, which takes the traveller within a short distance of Pembroke.

On leaving Portage du Fort in the steamer, we soon arrive at the Rapides Les Chenaux ; the river is here divided by small islands. covered with wood, between which the water rushes with great swiftness, but except in the high water of the spring, the steamer breasts the current gallantly ; the Chenaux Rapids are at the head of Lake Les Chats, a beautiful expansion of the river. Into Lake Les Chats are discharged, on the Ontario side, the River Bonne Chère, about 110 miles in lengths ; draining an area of 980 square miles ; the Madawaska, one of the largest of the tributaries, 210 miles in length, draining an area of 4,100 square miles ; on its mouth is situated the large and important village of Arnprior which has been created within a few years past by the liberal enterprise of Daniel McLachlan, Esquire; and the Mississippi, 101 miles long, draining an area of 1,150 miles. These are three of the largest timber producing tributaries of the Upper Ottawa.

Lake Les Chats is about 16 miles long, and is from 1 to 4 miles broad. There is a number of small islands scattered over its placid surface, and the lake being perfectly straight, these can be seen all at once.

The navigation of the River Ottawa is again totally arrested at the foot of Lake Les Chats, by a series of remarkable rapids, from which the Lake derives its name. The whole volume of water in this great river, here not far from a mile wide, is barred in a diagonal direction by a huge ledge of limestone rock, over which the water pours in white foam, and with stunning noise, from a height of 50 feet in 33 distinct falls in high water, and 16 when the water is low during summer. These falls are separated by Islands. Many of these cataracts are highly picturesque ; over every one of them there pours a volume of water, at least equal to that contained in the Teign, Dart, or Tavy, in Devonshire, five miles from their mouths. If in England, each separate cascade would attract as many visitors as the celebrated falls of Lodore, which is a mere rain-water spout compared with Les Chats. These falls can all be seen at once, as the steamer passes slowly along them, from Fitzroy Harbour, Ontario side, to the wharf at the other extremity of the falls on the Quebec side. The rocks between the Cascades are all covered with trees, many of them of large size, which gives them the appearence of Isiands.

On landing from the steamer at the foot of Lake Chats, we find ourselves on a convenient wharf, and presently we are invited to take a seat in an open carriage, drawn by two horses, and soon find ourselves travelling at a fast trot along a Railway track. This Railway is built across the barrier of rock on piles of squarred trees laid across each other in alternate layers; in many places, it has been necessary to raise these piles 20 feet from the ground, so as to obtain a level ; there is no railing or fence, but during the many years it has been in operation, no accident has ever occured on it. On arriving at the other end of the railroad, which is three miles long, we have a long flight of stairs to descend to the wharf below ; these are built in a wharehouse belonging to the steamboat company, and are necessary on account of the difference between the level of the railroad, and that of the river below.

Alongside of the wharf below lies the steamer on which we embark and steam at a rapid pace down the beautiful Lake Duchêne to Aylmer, a nice village on the Quebec side, only 8 miles from the City of Ottawa. The steamer stays at Aylmer on account of several rapids below, and passengers are brought into Ottawa by stages.

On the south side, below the Chats Rapids, is the mouth of the Carp, a small stream, at the village of Fitzroy Harbour, and almost opposite on the north side is the mouth of the Quio, also a small stream, but very important as it produces magnificent white pine.

The Chaudière Lake is about 30 miles long, winding southward towards its upper end, and is from 1 to 2 miles in breadth. Some of the lands, for 10 or 12 miles, on the Ontario side, are very good and well cultivated. Beyond this, and towards the Chats, the south coast is low and the soil not so good, being light and sandy, but is very superior a little further back ; on the Quebec shore the soil is also excellent, and on the road from Ottawa to Aylmer and above it. For a great part of the way the Eardley Mountains rise like a gigantic wall on the north side at four miles back from the lake.

At a short distance below Aylmer the Ottawa begins to close in and the stream becomes rapid and turbulent. The navigation is here interrupted again, for more than 5 miles, in which we find three short but distinct rapids, the Du Chêne, the Remnoks, and the little Chaudière ; these rapids have together a descent of about 60 feet over a bed of dark limestone, until at length the mighty stream pours in thunder over the rocks which arrest its progress at the City of Ottawa, forming the well known Chaudière Falls.

At the easterly boundary of the City, the Rideau pours over a high rocky bank into the Ottawa, on the Ontario side ; this river has a westerly course for 116 miles, and drains an area of 1,350 square miles.

About a mile lower down, on the Quebec side, is the mouth of the Gatineau, the largest of all the known tributaries, itself receiving tributaries, which would be called great rivers in any other country but this; one of them, the Jean de Terre, is known to have a course of 170 miles. The Gatineau is tolerably well known for about 200 miles of its course, but the remainder, supposed to be 240 miles more, penetrates into the unknown northern forests. At 217 miles from its mouth, the furthest point surveyed, the Gatineau is still a noble stream, at least 1,000 feet wide, diminished in depth, but little in width. The Gatineau is supposed to drain an area of 12,000 square miles, and from the great volumes of its waters, no doubt discharges those proceeding from some large inland lakes.

A small river, La Blanche, is discharged at a few miles below the Gatineau, and again a few miles below that is the mouth of the River aux Lièvres, having a course of about 260 miles, and connected with a chain of small lakes, which are themselves connected with the River St. Maurice, another large river which unites with the St Lawrence at the City of Three Rivers, half way between Montreal and Quebec.

The next tributary is the North Nation, and almost opposite, on the Ontario side, the South Nation, each stream having a course of about 100 miles.

Below the North Nation is the mouth of the River Rouge, with a course of 90 miles, and below that the River du Nord, with a course of 160 miles. No tributaries now occur until at a quite short distance from the mouth of the northern branch of the Ottawa, below Montreal, where it receives the River L'Assomption.

From the City of Ottawa, the river is navigable to Grenville, 63 miles below, where the navigation is interrupted by a rapid 12 miles long. This rapid is avoided by a canal constructed by the Imperial Government, but now in the hands of the Government of Canada, which is getting it enlarged to permit a larger class of vessels to pass through. At Grenville there is a Railway who takes passengers down to Carillon. On leaving the cars at Carillon the traveller finds himself steaming down the Ottawa, and there is no further obstruction to the navigation, except the short rapid at St. Anne's, which is avoided by one lock, on the north side ; the steamer then proceeds till the point is reached, at which the confluence of one of the outlets of the Ottawa with the St. Lawrence takes place, forming Lake St. Louis. The passengers disembark at Lachine, and Montreal is reached by rail.

The main stream of the Ottawa is divided into three, by the intervention of Isle Jésus and the Island of Montreal ; the north branch is the channel by which the lumber from the Ottawa finds its way to Quebec. The waters of the Ottawa are not finally merged into those of the St. Lawrence, until the junction of the two northern branches, at Bout de l'Isle, 130 miles from the city of Ottawa.

It is evident that the most prominent characteristic of the Ottawa is its great volume ; and in the spring, when the waters of the river are at their highest, from the rains and the melting of the northern snow, an approximate calculation shows that the volume of water passing over the Chaudière Falls, is equal to that of the Niagara Falls.

Many small streams and creeks which empty themselves into the Ottawa have not been mentioned, but if fourteen only of the best known tributaries are taken, it will be seen that they contain more than 3,000 miles of course, and drain an immense area of Country. Many of these tributaries are longer than many of the longest and largest of the rivers in Great Britain, and any one of them flowing in a country of the old world, would, long ere this, have become famous in song, in story, and in art.

In a general view the Valley of the Ottawa, is a region eight times the extent of Vermont, ten times that of Massachussetts ; it is drained by a noble river equal to the Rhine in its length of course, and to the Danube in magnitude ; the greater part of this noble valley is covered with a luxuriant growth of forest trees, particularly of red and white pine ; the harder wood also exists in abundance ; the soil is in general of excellent quality, and all the townships bordering on the river, and back on the course of several of the tributaries, are mostly settled.

Of the glorious forest scenery, it is hardly necessary to speak, for every one has heard of it ; there may be more beauty of form in the graceful and feathery palm, in the fragrant magnolia, the boast of tropic climes, but whether in the stern and gloomy grandeur of the pine forests, or in the exquisite beauty of colouring that distinguishes the hard wood groves when autumnal frosts have lighted up their leaves with all the splendours of crimson and gold, or a combination of them all, when the dark green foliage of the pines forms a background to the scarlet maples ; then, there is nothing in nature more grand than a Canadian forest in the autumn tide.

The tourists from the States wishing to visit the Ottawa Valley with its beauties, the usual pleasure route is *viâ* Saratoga, Niagara, down to Prescott, opposite Ogdensburg, N. Y., passing through the Thousand Islands. Prescott is the Terminus of the Ottawa and Prescott Railway. This Railroad makes two trips every day, to Ottawa and back, thus affording to travellers an expeditious and safe route, for this road is acknowledged to be the best built road in the country ; and like every other Railway and Steamboat Company in the Country, the employees are very attentive and obliging.

After visiting the principal places in the immediate vicinity of the City, the tourist leaves early in the morning, and after one hour's drive over a very good macadamized road, reaches the Village of Aylmer, and there finds the steamer ready to leave for the head of Lake Du Chêne ; the Railway takes him to the foot of Lake Chats, another steamer lies in waiting to take passengers up to Portage du Fort, (passing on the way, the beautiful Chenaux.) Here, if he does not wish to go further, he can put up at the Hotel for the night, and have ample time to look at the Rapids of the Grand Calumet ; see the timber passing through the slides ; collect some specimens of mica, combined with felspar, quartz, and of the fine white or pink statuary marble to be found in every direction ; a long night rest ; and return by the same steamer next morning. Should the tourist's time admit of it, we would by all means recommend him to continue his excursion upwards by the Grand Calumet route. From Portage du Fort there is an excellent macadamised road, seven miles in length, through a beautiful country, to the Grand Calumet. From the Calumet the steamer runs thirty miles, up the Calumet and Culbute Channels to within a few miles of Pembroke, to which the passengers are carried by a short stage and ferry. This route which passes up the channels on the north side of the Calumet and Allumette Islands and through Lake Coulonge, which lies between them, presents a series of richly, beautiful and romantic scenery surpassing any thing on the course of the Ottawa below it ; and only itself surpassed in beauty and grandeur, by the sail through Upper Allumette Lake and Deep River from Pembroke to the Deux Joachim. Sometimes the Calumet Steamer passes up the channel south of Allumette Island and Lower Allumette Lake to the Allumette Rapids below Pembroke. In returning down Paquet's Rapids, on this route the scenery and the panoramic effect of it is much finer than any thing that can be seen on the rapids of the St. Lawrence.

The other plan is to stop at Gould's wharf on the other side of the river, some distance before reaching Portage du Fort, take .the waggon in waiting and drive over the Portage to Muskrat Lake, where is a small steamer, which, with another short waggon portage, will bring him to Pembroke; there he will sleep ; from this another steamer will take him on to Les Deux Joachim, where in a most hospitable Hotel, he will find himself perfectly at home, and at the extremity of civilization. If he be indifferent to the fatigue of paddling or portaging, dangers of rapids, and a liking for pork and biscuit— he can go on to see the wild Rocher Capitaine, the Deux Rivières, the Cave, and the Montagne, see the beautiful fall of the Notawissi, pass the mouth of the Mysterious Keepawa-sippi, and make his camp-fire at the head of Temiscaming.

Returning down the River, were splendid pike fishing is to be had, and an occasional salmon trout, the tourist will, if he wish to go west, meet the train either at Sand point, the terminus of the Brock-ville Railroad, or proceed five miles further to Arnprior, from where the cars start daily for Brockville. But if he wish to go East he must return to Ottawa ; there he has to choose between the river Ottawa or the St. Lawrence. If he came to Ottawa by the O. and P. Rail-way from Prescott or Ogdensburg, he can take the steamer and pro-ceed down the Ottawa River to Grenville, then take the train to Car-rillon ;—arrived at Carillon, a steamer will take him to Lachine. Between Carillon and Lachine the navigation is interrupted by the rapids Ste. Anne, in reference to which Tom Moore wrote his admired Canadian boat song,

> " Row, brothers, row, the stream runs fast,
> " The rapids are near, and the day light is past, &c."

On its downwards trip, the steamer passes through the rapids Ste. Anne, then continues down the Ottawa, through the Lake of Two Mountains, to Lachine ; thence by Railway to Montreal, arriving at Montreal the same evening. The tourist will find this route very rich in scenery. But should he wish to descend the rapids of the St. Lawrence to Montreal, he can go by the Prescott and Ottawa Rail-way to Prescott, and take the downward boat ;—this route will take him through the Rapids les Galops, Rapid Plats, Long Sault, Les Cèdres, the Cascades, and Sault St. Louis, and when arrived at Mont-real, the tourist will admit that such sensation is not to be picked up everywhere. But if he does not wish to go to Montreal, he can cross over to Ogdensburg from Prescott, and proceed by Railway to Boston, New York, or any other place in the United States.

From Montreal, the tourist may reach Quebec by steamer or by Railway. Once in Quebec the sightseeker will convince himself that the old Stadacona is not below the fame she possesses of being the most Grand in scenery : we have heard a tourist say, that the view from Cap Diamond is, alone, worth the journey. The St. Lawrence watering places, deserve, also, the attention of the traveller. Rivière du Loup, Murray Bay, Tadoussac and the Saguenay, are places where he will find good society during the Summer months.

Returning to Quebec, he can take the route to the White Mountains, and then go southward, either by Portland or by the Railways. Thus the traveller may make a large circuit, without going twice over the same ground, or at least not much of it.

INTERNATIONAL CONVENTIONS

Of Delegates of the Legislatures of Canada, Nova Scotia, New Brunswick, Prince Edward's Island and Newfoundland, to settle the Basis of a Union of the British North American Provinces:

Convention held at Charlottetown 1st September, 1864.

CANADA.

The Honorable J. A. Macdonald, Attorney General, Upper Canada,
The Honorable George Brown, President of the Council,
The Honorable A. T. Galt, Finance Minister,
The Honorable G. E. Cartier, Attorney General, Lower Canada,
The Honorable Wm. McDougall, Provincial Secretary,
The Honorable Thomas D'Arcy McGee, Minister of Agriculture,
The Honorable H. L. Langevin, Solicitor General, Lower Canada.

NOVA SCOTIA.

The Honorable Chas. Tupper, Provincial Secretary,
The Honorable W. A. Henry, Attorney General,
The Honorable R. B. Dickie, Member of the Legislative Council,
The Honorable J. McCully, Member of the Legislative Council,
The Honorable A. G. Archibald, Member of the Provincial Parliament.

NEW BRUNSWICK.

The Honorable S. L. Tilley, Provincial Secretary,
The Honorable J. M. Johnston, Attorney General,
The Honorable J. H. Gray, M. P. P.,
The Honorable E. B. Chandler, M. L. C.,
The Honorable W. H. Steeves, M. L. C.

PRINCE EDWARD ISLAND.

The Honorable Colonel Gray, President of the Council,
The Honorable E. Palmer, Attorney General,
The Honorable W. H. Pope, Colonial Secretary,
The Honorable G. Coles, M. P. P.,
A. A. McDonald, M. L. C.

Convention held at Quebec, 10th October, 1864.

CANADA.

The Honorable Sir E. P. Taché, Receiver General and Minister of Militia,
The Honorable J. A. Macdonald, Attorney General, C. W.,
The Honorable George E. Cartier, Attorney General, C. E.,
The Honorable George Brown, President of Executive Council,
The Honorable O. Mowatt, Postmaster General,
The Honorable A. T. Galt, Minister of Finance,
The Honorable J. C. Chapais, Commissioner of Public Works,
The Honorable H. L. Langevin, Solicitor General, C. E.,
The Honorable J. Cockburn, Solicitor General, C. W.

NOVA SCOTIA.

The Honorable C. Tupper, Provincial Secretary,
The Honorable W. A. Henry, Attorney General,
The Honorable J. McCully, M. L. C., Leader of the Opposition,
The Honorable R. B. Dickey, M. P. P.,
The Honorable A. G. Archibald, M. P. P.

NEW BRUNSWICK.

The Honorable S. L. Tilley, Provincial and Financial Secretary,
The Honorable W. H. Steeves, Member of the Executive Council,
The Honorable J. M. Johnson, Attorney General,
The Honorable E. B. Chandler, M. L. C.,
Lieut.-Colonel Hon. J. H. Gray, M. P. P.,
The Honorable C. Fisher, M. P. P.

NEWFOUNDLAND.

The Honorable F. B. T. Carter, Speaker of the Legislative Assembly,
The Honorable J. A. Shea, Leader of the Opposition.

PRINCE EDWARD ISLAND.

Col. the Honorable W. H. Gray, Leader of the Government,
The Honorable E. Palmer, Attorney General,
The Honorable W. H. Pope, Provincial Secretary,
The Honorable A. A. McDonald, M. L. C.,
The Honorable G. Coles, M. P. P., Leader of the Opposition,
The Honorable J. H. Haviland, M. P. P.,
The Honorable E. Whelan, M. P. P.

Lt.-Colonel Hewitt Bernard, Secretary.

CONVENTION HELD AT LONDON (ENGLAND,)

Of Delegates to draft a Bill for the Union of Canada, Nova Scotia and New Brunswick, December, 1866.

CANADA.

The Honorable John Alexander Macdonald, Attorney General of Upper Canada and Minister of Militia of Canada —Chairman.
The Honorable George Etienne Cartier, Attorney General of Lower Canada.
The Honorable Alexander Tilloch Galt.
The Honorable William MacDougall, Secretary of the Province of Canada.
The Honorable William Pearce Howland, Minister of Finance.
The Honorable Hector L. Langevin, Postmaster General.

NOVA SCOTIA.

The Honorable Charles Tupper, M. D. Secretary of the Province.
The Honorable W. A. Henry, Attorney General.
The Honorable J. W. Ritchie, Solicitor General.
The Honorable Jonathan McCully.
The Honorable Adams G. Archibald.

NEW BRUNSWICK.

The Honorable Peter Mitchell, President of Council.
The Honorable R. D. Wilmot.
The Honorable Samuel L. Tilley, Secretary of the Province.
The Honorable Charles Fisher, Attorney General.
The Honorable J. M. Johnson.

Lt.-Colonel Hewitt Bernard, Secretary.

DOMINION OF CANADA.

GOVERNOR GENERAL OF THE DOMINION OF CANADA.

His Excellency the Right Honorable CHARLES STANLEY VISCOUNT MONCK, Baron Monck of Ballytrammon, in the County of Wexford, in the Peerage of Ireland, and Baron Monck of Ballytrammon, in the County of Wexford, in the Peerage of the United Kingdom of Great Britain and Ireland.

STAFF.

Denis Godley, Governor's Secretary.
Lieut.-Col. Hon. Richard Monck, Coldstream Guards, Military Secretary and Principal Aide-de-Camp.
Captain W. L. Pemberton, 60th Royal Rifles, Aide-de-Camp.
Lieut.-Col. I. G. Irvine, Canadian Militia, Provincial Aide-de-Camp.
Lieut.-Col. Philip Duchesnay, Canadian Militia, Extra Provincial Aide-de-Camp.
Lieut.-Col. Hewitt Bernard, Major Civil Service Rifle Volunteers, Extra Provincial Aide-de-Camp.
Lieut.-Col. F. W. Cumberland, late 10th Royals (Volunteers) Toronto, Extra Provincial Aide-de-Camp.

PRIVY COUNCILLORS FOR THE DOMINION OF CANADA.

The Honorable Sir JOHN ALEXANDER MACDONALD, K. C. B., Minister of Justice and Attorney General,

The Honorable GEORGE ETIENNE CARTIER, Minister of Militia,

The Honorable SAMUEL LEONARD TILLEY, C. B., Minister of Customs,

The Honorable JOHN ROSE Minister of Finance,

The Honorable WILLIAM McDOUGALL, C. B., Minister of Public Works,

The Honorable WILLIAM PEARCE HOWLAND, C. B., Minister of Inland Revenue,

The Honorable ADAMS GEORGE ARCHIBALD, Secretary of State for the Provinces,

The Honorable ADAM JOHNSTON FERGUSSON BLAIR, President of the Privy Council,

The Honorable PETER MITCHELL, Minister of Marine and Fisheries,

The Honorable ALEXANDER CAMPBELL, Postmaster General,

The Honorable JEAN CHARLES CHAPAIS, Minister of Agriculture,

The Honorable HECTOR LOUIS LANGEVIN, Secretary of State of Canada,

The Honorable EDWARD KENNY, Receiver General.

W. H. LEE, Clerk,
W. A. HIMSWORTH, Ass. Clerk.

LIEUT.-GOVERNORS OF THE PROVINCES IN THE DOMINION OF CANADA.

Ontario :—Major-General HENRY WILLIAM STISTED, C. B.
Quebec:—The Honorable Sir NARCISSE FORTUNAT BELLEAU, Knight.

Nova Scotia:—Major General CHARLES HASTINGS DOYLE.
New Brunswick :— Colonel FRANCIS PYM. HARDING, C. B.

EXECUTIVE COUNCIL OF THE PROVINCE OF ONTARIO.

The Honorable J. S. MACDONALD, Attorney General and Prime Minister,
The Honorable STEPHEN RICHARDS, Commissioner of Crown Lands,
The Honorable M. C. CAMERON, Q. C., Provincial Secretary and Registrar,

The Honorable E. B. WOOD, Treasurer,
The Honorable JOHN CARLING, Commissioner of Agriculture and Public Works.

EXECUTIVE COUNCIL OF THE PROVINCE OF QUEBEC.

The Honorable PIERRE JOSEPH OLIVIER CHAUVEAU, Secretary and Registrar,
The Honorable GÉDÉON OUIMET, Attorney General,
The Honorable CHRISTOPHER DUNKIN, Treasurer,

The Honorable JOSEPH OCTAVE BEAUBIEN, Commissioner of Crown Lands,
The Honorable LOUIS ARCHAMBAULT, Commissioner of Agriculture and Public Works,
The Honorable GEORGE IRVINE, Solicitor General.

EXECUTIVE COUNCIL OF THE PROVINCE OF NEW BRUNSWICK.

The Honorable A. R. WETMORE, Attorney General,
The Honorable J. A. BECKWITH, Provincial Secretary,
The Honorable RICHARD SUTTON, Surveyor General,
The Honorable JOHN McADAM, Chief Commissioner Public Works,

The Honorable C. N. SKINNER, Solicitor General,
The Honorable A. C. DES BRISAY, (without Department.)
The Honorable BENJAMIN BEVERIDGE, (without Department.)
The Honorable JAMES P. FLEWELLING, (without Department.)

EXECUTIVE COUNCIL OF THE PROVINCE OF NOVA SCOTIA.

The Honorable W. ARMAND, Treasurer,
The Honorable M. VAIL, Provincial Secretary.
The Honorable R. ROBERTSON, Commissioner of Mines,
The Honorable MARTIN J. WILKINS, Attorney General,

The Honorable R. McHEFFEY, President of the Council.
The Honorable M. TROOP, (without Department.)

—

E. M. MACDONALD, Queen's Printer.

MEMBERS OF THE SENATE OF CANADA.

The Honorable JOSEPH CAUCHON, Speaker.

For the Province of Ontario :

Hon. John Hamilton, Kingston,
" Roderick Matheson, Perth,
" John Ross, Toronto,
" Samuel Mills, Hamilton,
" Benjamin Seymour, Port Hope,
" Walter H. Dickson, Niagara,
" James Shaw, Smith's Falls,
" Adam J. Fergusson Blair, Guelph,
" Alexander Campbell, Kingston,
" David Christie, Paris,
" James Cox Aikins, Richview,
" David Reesor, Markham,

Hon. Elijah Leonard, London,
" William MacMaster, Toronto,
" Asa Allworth Burnham, Cobourg,
" John Simpson, Bowmanville,
" James Skead, Ottawa,
" David L. Macpherson, Toronto,
" George Crawford, Brockville,
" Donald Macdonald, Toronto,
" Oliver Blake, Waterford,
" Billa Flint, Belleville,
" Walter McCrea, Chatham,
" George William Allan, Toronto.

For the Province of Quebec :

Hon. James Leslie, Montreal,
" Asa B. Foster, Waterloo, P. Q.,
" Joseph Noël Bossé, Quebec,
" Louis A. Olivier, Berthier,
" Jacques Oliv. Bureau, Montreal,
" Charles Malhiot, Pointe du Lac,
" Louis Renaud, Montreal,
" Luc Letellier de St. Just, Rivière
   Ouelle,
" Ulric Joseph Tessier, Quebec,
" John Hamilton, Hawkesbury,
" Charles Cormier, Plessisville, So-
   merset,
" Antoine Juchereau Duchesnay,
   Ste. Catherine de Fossambault,
" David Edward Price, Chicoutimi,

Hon. Elzear H. J. Duchesnay, Ste Ma-
   rie, N. Beauce,
" Leandre Dumouchel, Ste. Thérèse
   de Blainville,
" Louis Lacoste, Boucherville,
" Joseph F. Armand, Riv. des Prai-
   ries,
" Charles Wilson, Montreal,
" William Henry Chaffers, St. Cé-
   saire,
" Jean Bte. Guévremont, Sorel,
" James Ferrier, Montreal,
Sir Narcisse Fortunat Belleau, Knight,
   Quebec,
Hon. Thomas Ryan, Montreal,
" John Sewall Sanborn, Sherbrooke.

For the Province of Nova Scotia :

Hon. Edward Kenny, Halifax,
" Jonathan McCully, do.
" Thomas D. Archibald, Sydney,
   C. B.,
" Robt. B. Dickey, Amherst, C. C.,
" John H. Anderson, Halifax,
" John Holmes, East River, Pictou,

Hon. John W. Ritchie, Halifax,
" Benjamin Wier, do.
" John Locke, Locke's Island, Shel-
   burne,
" Caleb R. Bill, Billtown, K. C.,
" John Bourinot, Sydney, C. B.
" William Miller, Halifax.

For the Province of New Brunswick :

Hon. Amos Edwin Botsford, Westcock,
   Westmorland,
" Edward Barron Chandler, Dor-
   chester, Westmorland,
" John Robertson, St. John, N. B.,
" Robert Leonard Hazen, do. do.,
" William Hunter Odell, Frederick-
   ton, York,
" David Wark, Richibucto, Kent,
" William Henry Steeves, St. John,
   N. B.,

Hon. William Todd, St. Stephen, Char-
   lotte,
" John Ferguson, Bathurst, Glou-
   cester,
" Robert Duncan Wilmot, Belmont,
   Sunbury,
" Abner Reid McClelan, Hopeville,
   Albert,
" Peter Mitchell, Newcastle, Nor-
   thumberland.

LEGISLATIVE COUNCILLORS.

For the Province of Quebec :

Hon. C. B. DeBoucherville, Speaker,
" John LeBoutillier,
" Elizée Dionne,
" Joseph Octave Beaubien,
" Alexandre Chaussegros de Léry,
" Isidore Thibaudeau,
" Jean Baptiste George Proulx,
" Edward Hale,
" David Morrison Armstrong,
" Thomas Wood,
" John Fraser,
" Charles Séraphin Rodier,

Hon. Jean Elie Gingras,
" Louis Panet,
" Thomas McGreevy,
" John Jones Ross,
" Pierre Eustache Dostaler,
" Louis Archambault,
" Félix Hyacinthe Lemair,
" George Bryson,
" Jean Louis Beaudry,
" James Ferrier,
" Joseph Eustache Prud'homme,
" Henry Starnes.

For the Province of Nova Scotia:

Hon. Alexander Keith, Speaker,
" R. Mollison Cutler,
" Staley Brown,
" M. Byles Almon,
" Henry Gesner Pineo,
" J. McNab,
" R. A. McHeffey,
" J. Creighton,
" W. C. Whitman,
" Freeman Tupper,

Hon. Archibald Patterson,
" Samuel Chipman,
" McKean,
" Peter Smyth,
" John McKinnon,
" W. S. Heffernan,
" D. McN. Parker,
" Jas. Fraser,
" Samuel Creelman.

For the Province of New Brunswick:

Hon. T. S. Saunders, Speaker,
" E. B. Chandler,
" Wm. B. Kinnear,
" Geo. Minchin,
" Chas. Harrison,
" Jas. Davidson,
" J. H. Ryan,
" Wm. Hamilton,

Hon. William Todd,
" A. McL. Seely,
" Francis Rice,
" J. J. Robinson,
" Charles Perley,
" Mr. Muirhead,
" R. Young.

MEMBERS ELECTED FOR THE HOUSE OF COMMONS AND LOCAL LEGISLATURES.

Honorable JAMES COCKBURN, Speaker of the House of Commons.

Province of Ontario.

CONSTITUENCIES.	HOUSE OF COMMONS.	LOCAL LEGISLATURE.
Addington...............	J. N. Lapum..........	A. F. Hooper.
Algoma.................	W. M. Simpson........	Fred.W. Cumberland, Q. C.
Bothwell...............	D. Mills.............	A. McKellar.
Brockville	James Crawford......	Wm. Fitzsimmons.

NOTE.—The Parliament of the Dominion consists of the Queen, a Senate of 72, appointed by the Crown for life, and a House of Commons of 181 Members chosen by the People. The Members of this Parliament are locally apportioned as follows :—

	Senators.	Members of the H. of Commons.
For Ontario,	24	82
" Quebec,	24	65
" Nova Scotia,	12	19
" New Brunswick,	12	15

The number of Senators is fixed (except that six additional Senators may be appointed by the Crown) ; that of Members of the House of Commons is to vary according to population ascertained at each decennial census, Quebec retaining the same number. Thus, supposing the calculations in our article on the census [respecting gradual increase of population] to be correct, the House of Commons will be thus constituted after 1871: Ontario 98, Quebec 65, Nova Scotia 18, New Brunswick 15, total 196. Term of election, 5 years, unless the house be sooner dissolved. Sessions annual. The property qualification is : for Senators the possession of $4,000 real and personal estate over and above all liabilities ; for members of the House of Commons in Ontario and Quebec, £500 sterling of real estate ; in New Brunswick the possession for six months previous to the issue of the writ of election of $1,200 of real estate ; in Nova Scotia "a legal or equitable freehold estate in possession of the clear yearly value of eight dollars ($8)," or the candidate must be "qualified to be an elector."
The following are electors : In Ontario and Quebec, every male subject being the owner, or occupier, or tenant of real property of the assessed value of $300, or of the yearly value of $30, if within cities or towns, or of the assessed value of $200, or the yearly value of $20, if not so situate. In New Brunswick, every male subject of the age of 21 years, not disqualified by law, assessed for the year for which the register is made up, in respect of real estate to the amount of $100 or of personal property or personal and real amounting together to $400, or $400 annual income. In Nova Scotia, all subjects of the age of 21 years, not disqualified by law, assessed for the year for which the register is made up in respect of real estate to the value of $150, or in respect of personal estate or of real and personal together to the value of $300.
Voting in Quebec, Ontario and Nova Scotia is open, on enquiry by the Returning Officers, after the person desirous of voting has by reference to the registration list established his right to vote. In New Brunswick votes are taken by ballot.—B. N. A. Year Book, 1868.

Province of Ontario.—Continued.

CONSTITUENCIES.	HOUSE OF COMMONS.	LOCAL LEGISLATURE.
Brant North	J. Y. Bown	Hugh Finlayson.
Brant South	Hon. E. B. Wood	Hon. E. B. Wood, Q. C.
Bruce North	Alex. Sproat	Donald Sinclair.
Bruce South	Francis Hurdon	E. Blake, Q. C.
Carleton	John Holmes	Robert Lyon.
Cornwall	Hon. J. S. Macdonald	Hon. J. S. Macdonald, Q. C.
Cardwell	T. R. Ferguson	T. Swinarton.
Dundas	John S. Ross	Simon Cook.
Durham East	F. H. Burton	A. T. H. Williams.
Durham West	E. Blake	—— McLeod.
Essex	John O'Connor	Solomon Wigle.
Elgin West	J. H. Munro	Nicoll McCall.
Elgin East	T. W. Dobbie	D. Luton.
Frontenac	T. Kirkpatrick	Sir Henry Smith.
Grey South	George Jackson	A. W. Lauder.
Grey North	George Snider	Thomas Scott.
Glengarry	D. A. Mcdonald	James Craig.
Grenville South	Walter Shanly	W. McNeil Clarke.
Hamilton	Charles Magill	J. M Williams.
Hastings West	James Brown	K. Graham.
Hastings East	Hon. Robt. Read	Henry Corby.
Halton	John White	Wm. Barber.
Haldimand	D. Thompson	J. Baxter.
Hastings North	McKenzie Bowell	J. H. Boulton.
Huron North	J. Whitehead	W. T. Hayes.
Huron South	M. C. Cameron	R. Gibbons.
Kingston	Hon. Sir Jno. A. Macdonald, K. C. B	Maxwell W. Strange.
Kent	Rufus Stephenson	John Smith.
London	Hon. J. Carling	Hon. J. Carling.
Lincoln	Hon. Jas. R. Benson	J. C. Rykert.
Lanark North	Hon W. McDougall, C.B.	David Galbraith.
Lanark South	Alex. Morris	W. McNairn Shaw.
Lennox	R. J. Cartwright	J. Stevenson.
Leeds (N.) and Grenville	Francis Jones	Henry D. Smith.
Leeds South	John Crawford	Benjamin Tett.
Lambton	Alex. MacKenzie	J. B. Pardee.
Monck	L. McCallum	George Secord.
Middlesex North	Thos. Scatchard	J. S. Smith.
Middlesex West	A. P. Mcdonald	M. Currie.
Middlesex East	Crowell Wilson	Jas. Evans.
Norfolk North	Aquila Walsh	James Wilson.
Norfolk South	P. Lawson	S. McCall.
Northumberland E	Joseph Keeler	John Eyre.
Northumberland W	Honble. J. Cockburn	A. Fraser.
Niagara	Angus Morrison	D. Robertson.
Ottawa City	J. M. Currier	R. W. Scott, Q. C.
Ontario South	T. N. Gibbs	Dr. McGill.
Ontario North	J. H. Thompson	Thomas Paxton.
Oxford North	Thomas Oliver	George Perry.
Oxford South	E. V. Bodwell	Adam Oliver.
Peterboro' East	P. M. Grover	George Read.

Province of Ontario.—Continued.

CONSTITUENCIES.	HOUSE OF COMMONS.	LOCAL LEGISLATURE.
Peterboro' West	Charles Perry	John Carnegie, Jr.
Prescott	Albert Hagar	James Boyd.
Perth North	J. Redford	A. Monteith.
Perth South	R. MacFarlane	James Trow.
Prince Edward	Walter Ross	A. Greely.
Peel	Hon. J. H. Cameron	John Coyne.
Russell	J. A. Grant	Wm. Craig.
Renfrew North	John Rankin	John Supple, Senr.
Renfrew South	D. McLachlin	J. L. Macdougall.
Simcoe South	W. C. Little	T. R. Ferguson.
Simcoe North	T. D. McConkey	W. Lount.
Stormont	Samuel Ault	Wm. Colquhoun.
Toronto East	James Beaty	Hon. M. C. Cameron, Q. C.
Toronto West	R. A. Harrison	John Wallis.
Victoria South	G. Kempt	Thos. Matchett.
Victoria North	John Morrison	A. P. Cockburn.
Waterloo North	I. E. Bowman	Moses Springer.
Waterloo South	James Young	I. Clemens.
Welland	T. C. Street	William Beaty.
Wentworth South	Joseph Rymal	William Sexton.
Wentworth North	Jas. McMonies	Robert Christie.
Wellington North	George A. Drew	Robert McKim.
Wellington Centre	T. S. Parker	A. D. Ferrier.
Wellington South	David Stirton	Peter Gow.
York West	Hon. W. P. Howland, C. B.	T. Graham.
York East	James Metcalfe	H. P. Crosby.
York North	James P. Wells	Hon. J. McMurrich.

Province of Quebec.

Argenteuil	Hon. J. J. C. Abbott	S. Bellingham.
Bagot	P. S. Gendron	P. S. Gendron.
Beauce	C. H. Pozer	C. H. Pozer.
Beauharnois	M. Cayley	Célestin Bergevin.
Bellechasse	N. Casault	Dr. Onésime Peltier.
Berthier	A. H. Paquet	Louis Joseph Moll.
Bonaventure	T. Robitaille	Clarence Hamilton.
Brome	Hon. C. Dunkin	Hon. C. Dunkin.
Chambly	B. Benoit	Jean-Baptiste Jodoin.
Champlain	J. J. Ross	J. J. Ross.
Charlevoix	S. X. Cimon	Léon Charles Clément.
Chateauguay	Hon. L. H. Holton	Edouard Laberge.
Chicoutimi and Saguenay	P. A. Tremblay	P. A. Tremblay.
Compton	J. H. Pope	James Ross.
Dorchester	Hon. H. L. Langevin	Hon. H. L. Langevin.
Drummond & Arthabaska	L. A. Sénécal	Edward John Hemming.
Gaspé	P. Fortin	P. Fortin.
Hochelaga	Hon. A. A. Dorion	Louis J. B. Beaubien.
Huntingdon	Hon. John Rose	Julius Scriver.

DIAGRAM OF THE HOUSE OF COMMONS.

THE SPEAKER.

Province of Quebec.—Continued.

CONSTITUENCIES.	HOUSE OF COMMONS.	LOCAL LEGISLATURE.
Iberville	F. Béchard	Louis Molleur.
Jacques Cartier	G. G. Gaucher	Narcisse M. Lecavalier.
Joliette	F. B. Godin	Vincent Paul Lavallée.
Kamouraska		
Laprairie	A. Pinsonnault	Césaire Thérien.
L'Assomption	Hon. L. Archambault	Et. Mathieu.
Laval	J. H. Bellerose	J. H. Bellerose.
Lévis	J. G. Blanchet	J. G. Blanchet.
L'Islet	B. Pouliot	Pamphile G. Verrault.
Lotbinière	H. G. Joly	H. G. Joly.
Maskinongé	G. Caron	Alexis Lesieur Desaulniers.
Megantic	Hon. G. Irvine	Hon. G. Irvine.
Missisquoi	B. Chamberlin	Josiah Sanford Brigham.
Montcalm	Jos. Dufresne	Firmin Dugas.
Montmagny	Hon. J. O. Beaubien	Louis Henry Blais.
Montmorency		
Montreal (City) W.	Hon. D'Arcy McGee	Alex. Walker O'Gilvie.
Montreal (City) C	Thomas Workman	Edward Carter.
Montreal (City) E	Hon. G. E. Cartier	Hon. G. E. Cartier.
Napierville	S. Coupal	Pierre Benoit.
Nicolet	Jos. Gaudet	Jos. Gaudet.
Ottawa (County)	A. Wright	Levi Ruggles Church.
Pontiac	Edmund Heath	John Poupore.
Portneuf	J. T. Brousseau	Dr. Praxède Larue.
Quebec (City) E.	P. G. Huot	J. P. Rhéaume.
Quebec (City) W.	Thos. McGreavy	John Hearn.
Quebec (City) C.	G. H. Simard	G. H. Simard.
Quebec (County)	Hon. P. J. O. Chauveau	Hon. P. J. O. Chauveau.
Richmond and Wolfe	W. H. Webb	Jacques Picard.
Richelieu	T. McCarthy	Joseph Baudreau.
Rimouski	G. Sylvain	Joseph Garon.
Rouville	G. Cheval dit St. Jacques	V. Robert.
St. Hyacinthe	Hon. E. A. Kierzkowski	P. Bachand.
St. John's	François Bourassa	F. G. Marchand.
St. Maurice	L. L. L. Desaulniers	L. A. Desaulniers.
Shefford	Hon. L. S. Huntington	Michel Adrien Bessette.
Sherbrooke (Town)	Hon A. T. Galt	Joseph Gibb Robertson.
Soulanges	L. H. Masson	Dominique A. Coutlée.
Stanstead	Chs. C. Colby	Thomas Locke.
Témiscouata	C. F. A. Bertrand	Elie Mailloux.
Terrebonne	L. F. R. Masson	J. A. Chapeleau.
Three Rivers (City)	C. B. deNiverville	C. B. deNiverville.
Two Mountains	J. B. D'Aoust	Hon. G. Ouimet.
Vaudreuil	D. McMillan	{ A. C. DeLotbinière Harwood.
Verchères	F. Geoffrion	A. Boniface Craig.
Yamaska	Moïse Fortier	Louis Adélard Sénécal.

3

Province of Nova Scotia.

CONSTITUENCIES.	HOUSE OF COMMONS.	LOCAL LEGISLATURE.
Annapolis..............	W. H. Ray	J. C. Troop, D. C. Landers.
Antigonish.............	H. McDonald........	D. McDonald, J. McDonald.
Colchester.............	A. W. McClellan......	Robt. Chambers, T. F. Morrison.
Cumberland...........	Hon. C. Tupper, C. B..	Amos Purdy, H. G. Pineo.
Cape Breton...........	Hon. James McKeagny.	J. Ferguson, N. L. McKay.
Digby	A. W. Savary........	W. B. Vail, Mr. Doucette.
Guysborough...........	Hon. S. Campbell.....	Jno. J. Marshall, Jno. A. Kirke.
Halifax .... {	A. G. Jones........ } P. Power.......... }	H. Balcam, J. Cochran, Jer. Northup.
Hants	Hon. Jos. Howe.......	W. Laurence, E. Young.
Inverness	H. Cameron..........	Hon. H. Blanchard, A. Campbell.
King's	W. H. Chipman.......	D. M. Dickie, E. L. Brown.
Lunenburg.............	E. M. McDonald......	Jas. Eisenhaur, M. B. Des Brisay.
Pictou................	G. W. Carmichael.....	R. S. Copeland, M. J. Wilkins, Dr. Murray.
Queen's...............	J. F. Forbes.........	H. W. Smith, D. Freeman.
Richmond.............	W. G. Croke.........	E. P. Flynn, J. Hooper.
Shelburne............	Thos. Coffin.........	R. Robertson, Thos. Johnson.
Victoria	W. Ross.............	John Ross, W. Kidston.
Yarmouth.............	Hon. Thos. Killam....	J. K. Ryerson, W. H. Townsend.

Province of New Brunswick.

Albert	J. Wallace...........	Mr. Peck, Mr. Bliss.
Carleton	Hon. C. Connell......	W. Lindsay, J. E. Hartley.
Charlotte	J. Bolton	J. McAdam, A. Hibbard.
Gloucester	T. W. Anglin.........	J. Meahan, A. DesBrisay.
Kent	A. Renaud	Mr. Caie, Mr. McInerney.

Province of New Brunswick.—Continued.

CONSTITUENCIES.	HOUSE OF COMMONS.	LOCAL LEGISLATURE.
King's................	G. Ryan.............	{ N. P. Flewelling, J. Flewelling.
Northumberland........	Hon. J. M. Johnson...	Geo. Kerr, R. Sutton, W. Kelly, J. Gough.
Queen's..............	J. Ferris............	{ R. T. Babitt, W. S. Butler.
Restigouche..........	Hon. J. McMillan.....	J. Montgomery.
Sunbury..............	C. Purpee...........	{ J. Glazier, W. E. Perley.
Saint John (City & County)	Hon. J. H. Gray......	J. Pickard, Hon. A. R. Wetmore, C. N. Skinner, J. Quinton.
Saint John (City)........	Hon. S. L. Tilley, C. B..	
Victoria.............	J. Costigan..........	{ B. Beveridge, Mr. Hebert.
Westmoreland..........	Hon. A. J. Smith......	B. Betisford, A. McQueen, A. Landry.
York.................	Hon. C. Fisher.......	D. Hanington, J. Lewis, H. Dow, J. A. Beckwith, A. Thomson.

EXTRACT OF THE ROUTINE AND PRACTICE OF PARLIAMENT.

(By an old Member.)

———

AVOIDANCE OF A DECISION.—When a motion has been made, upon which the House is unwilling to come to a vote, there are certain formal modes of avoiding a decision, amongst which are—

"Passing to the other orders of the day."

"Moving the previous question."

The former means that the House should—casting aside and taking no further notice of the matter then before it—proceed to the other business appointed for that day; the latter means, that a vote be previously taken as to the expediency of coming to any decision on the question raised. If "*the previous question*" of expediency be negatived, the motion to which it referred is not killed—it is only delayed for a time ; but a direct negative to the motion itself, would proscribe it for the remainder of the Session, as well as deny the principle involved. With respect to a Bill,—by moving that it "*be read this day six months*," or "*this day three months*," it is thrown over without coming to any express declaration against the principle of the measure.

BILLS (*Public.*)—A Bill is the draft or skeleton of a Statute. No Bill can be brought in unless a motion for leave be previously agreed to, or upon motion to appoint a Committee to prepare and bring it in ; it is then brought in and read a first time, generally without amendment or debate; a day is then appointed for the second reading, before which day it is printed, and a copy furnished to every member. After the second reading, it is referred to a Committee of the whole House, when its details are considered, as its principles were, upon its previous readings. The principles of a Bill may be discussed at any of its stages, but no member is considered to have declared decisively in its favor, unless he supports it by his vote at the second reading. In Committee of the whole House, the preamble and title are the last considered. The Bill is debated or considered clause by clause. The blanks left for *names, dates, nature and amount of penalty*, are filled up while in Committee, and it frequently happens that the Bill is entirely re-modelled. Formerly the blanks were left, but now it is the practice to fill up those blanks with the proposed words printed in italics. It avoids surprise, and frequently discussion; for being before the members, they are agreed to without any questions being put, unless any member should propose to alter them. The Chairman of the Committee then makes a report to the House of the changes made to the Bill, which he does by presenting a copy of it to the Speaker in its altered form. The report is forthwith received, or ordered to be received on a certain day, and the Bill is still open for amendment and debate before the third reading; but when a Bill is reported without amendment, it is forthwith ordered to be read a third time at such time as may be appointed by the House. After a Bill has been read a third time, amendments may still be added; if a new clause be added, it is called a "Rider." The last question but one is, that "the Bill do pass." After this, nothing remains except to determine its title. During the progress of a Bill, the House may divide on the following questions :—

1st. On the Second Reading.
2nd. That it be committed.
3rd. That the Report of the Committee be received.
4th. That the Bill be recommitted.
5th. That it be read a Third Time.
6th. That it do pass.
7th. The title of the Bill.

These are exclusive of any divisions in Committee, or on any amendments, or clauses proposed to be added to or taken from the measure, in or out of the Committee. Alterations are not usually proposed to a Bill until after its principle has been disposed of, on the second reading. Immediately after the passing of the Bill, it is taken to the Upper House, and the concurrence of the Senate is asked thereto. If a Bill be rejected, no further proceedings ensue. When the Senate agree with the Commons on the principle of a measure, but differ in matters of detail, a conference sometimes follows, between Members deputed from each House, who generally succeed in adjusting the difference ; but if both Houses are inflexible, the Bill is dropped.

No Bill relating to trade, or the alteration of the Laws concerning trade, can be brought into the House, until the proposition shall have been first considered in committee of the whole House, and agreed to by the House. The same proceeding is required with reference to any new tax to be imposed upon the people of any locality.

THE BUDGET.—The Minister of Finance makes one general statement every year to the Commons, which is intended to present a comprehensive view of the financial condition of the country. It is not to be supposed that this is the only speech which the Minister of Finance is called upon to make; but this is the *speech*, shewing the past and giving his views upon the future, and in fact. it is a demand made upon the people's Representatives, to confirm his conduct in managing the Financial Department of the country. He courts enquiry, and expects to hear from the leader of the Opposition, his views upon the prospects of the material interests of the country, as laid before Parliament. Any changes which a Government propose to make in the financial position of the country, are always pointedly alluded to in this speech, and the Opposition is thus put in full possession of what the Government intend to do.

CLERK OF THE HOUSE OF COMMONS.—The Clerk of the Commons is certainly one of great office trust and importance. He is appointed by the Crown, and has the right of appointing his own deputy, when one is required. In England, the appointment of the other officers of the House is vested in the Clerk ; but it is different in Canada. Either the Speaker or the House, at the instance of the Committees, make the appointments. It is his duty to make minutes—not of the arguments held in the House, but of the decisions at which it arrives—in other words, simply to record its votes, resolutions. addresses. orders, reports, divisions, and all other proceedings in which it may be engaged ; to see that they are correctly printed, and distributed to the members; to read aloud all such documents as the House may order to be read ; to perform the duty (without taking the chair) of chairman during the choice of speaker. He has two assistants, who aid him in the despatch of the business, so that no delay may be occasioned.

COMMITTALS.--In common with Courts of Law and Equity, the Houses of Parliament can punish all contempts of their authority or disobedience of their mandates. Each House is armed with power to repress any aggression committed upon their rights, or any interference with their privileges; which, however, cease when Parliament is prorogued. The Commons, as well as the Senate, has the right to delegate to a Committee the power of sending for persons, records and papers, and of enforcing the attendance of necessary witnesses.

COMMITTEES.—Are, *first*, those of the whole House, which may be to consider certain Resolutions, as to the nature of which considerable latitude prevails : or the House resolves itself into Committee to consider the details of a Bill, the principle of which may be discussed at any or all of its other stages ; or there may be a Committee for financial purposes, as those of "Supply," or "Ways and Means," as alluded to elsewhere. *Secondly*.—There are Select Committees chosen by ballot or otherwise, for some specific purpose. The numbers composing such Committees vary according to the nature of the case, but cannot exceed fifteen, unless by permission of the House. *Finally*.—Election Committees, chosen in accordance with the Act of Parliament regulating controverted Elections. These Committees discharge the duties of judicial tribunals. They are appointed by a general Committee, on Elections, who, after having selected a certain number from the members to constitute the Chairmen's panel, divide the remainder into panels, and report the same to the House, marked 1, 2 and 3. The Clerk, in the presence of the House, places the whole three in a hat, and draws them forth, numbering each in rotation, A, B, C. The General Committee then selects four members for the Committee for the first controverted Election referred to them, and at the same time the Chairmen's panel assembles and ballots for a Chairman for the particular Committee chosen. Then there are several Standing Committees. When the whole House is in Committee, the Speaker vacates the Chair, the Mace is placed under the table, some member is called to preside, who occupies the seat of the senior Clerk. When Select Committees are appointed, no member who has declared against the principle or substance of a Bill, Resolution, or matter to be committed, can be nominated of such Committee.

CONFERENCE.—There is a species of negociation between the two Houses of Parliament, conducted by managers appointed by each, for the purpose of producing concurrence, in cases where mutual consent is necessary ; or for the purpose of reconciling differences which may have arisen upon any matter requiring the action of both Houses. If the conference be upon the subject of a Bill depending between the two Houses, it must be demanded by that House, which, at the time of asking the Conference, is in possession of the Bill. When the Commons requests a Conference with the Senate, the reasons to be given by the Commons must be prepared and agreed to by the House, before a message is sent to the Senate asking a Conference. These are furnished to the Managers, who on meeting the Managers of the Upper House, hand in the reasons in writing. Should this proceeding fail in its object, a "free Conference" is held, which gives an opportunity for the Managers individually, and unrestrained by any set form of argument, to urge such reasons as in their judgment may best tend to influence the House to which they are addressed. A free Conference is usually held, if two Conferences have been held without accomplishing the desired object. After one free Conference has been held upon any one subject, no other but a free Conference can be held touching the same topic. While the Managers of a Conference are absent on duty, the Speaker vacates the chair.

ESTATE OF PARLIAMENT.—Parliament fully assembled, consists of the Monarch, or his Representative, the Upper House, and the Lower House. They are more frequently spoken of as the three branches of the Legislature. Neither House deliberates in the presence of the Queen's Representative, nor will either of them permit any allusion, in debate, to the opinions or sentiments entertained by him. The three branches taken together, exercise none but legislative functions, and they must all consent, or no law can be passed. But they have separate functions as well. The Monarch, or Representative, holds the whole executive authority, and while the Lower House alone can originate Money or Tax Bills, the Upper House is deprived of this power. Nor does the Upper House possess the great function of trying impeachments, which is held by the Lords in Great Britain, from the simple fact, that there is no power invested with the right to impeach.

House of Commons.—The Speaker takes the chair at 3 P. M., daily. If there is a quorum, the business is proceeded with; if not, the House is adjourned till the next day, at 3 P. M. Early meetings take place at the close of the Session, in order to expedite business, and bring matters to a close. The House does not usually meet on Saturday, nor does it assemble on any holiday. No one can be admitted to hear the debates, without an order from the Sergeant-at-Arms, which is generally obtained through a Member. Twenty Members constitute a quorum.

Interruption of the Sittings of Parliament.—The proceedings of the Legislature may be interrupted or suspended either by ajournment, prorogation, or dissolution.

Adjournment, as the term itself implies, is a postponement of the sitting or proceedings of the House, from one time to another specified for the re-assemblage. When the sitting of both Houses are interrupted by royal authority, it is called prorogation. Dissolution puts an end to the representative character of the individuals who, at the time, compose the House of Commons, and Parliament cannot therefore assemble until after a new election, except in cases hereinafter mentioned. The power of adjournment is a right belonging to each House, and there are no restraints to this power.

The House of Commons can interrupt or postpone any debate, defer the consideration of any measure, or altogether adjourn its sitting, but the practice is always to adjourn to some stated time; and I think there can be no doubt that, by the previous permission of the House, the Speaker can leave the Chair for a certain number of hours; but this does not amount to an adjournment, and could not be noted as such by the Clerk. But it must be remarked that the adjournment of one House does not adjourn the other. The Crown may, pending an adjournment, summon by proclamation, either House, or both, and may direct either, or both Houses to adjourn to any particular day. But while this power exists, and although in former times it has been frequently exercised in the Imperial Legislature, it has grown into dissuetude there as well as in the provinces, enjoying the privileges of their own local Legislatures.

An individual member may for a time interrupt the progress of business by successive motions for adjournment, which may be repeated indefinitely, with this restriction: no second motion to adjourn can be made until after some intermediate proceeding shall have been had. The motion in committee that the chairman report progress, is equivalent to a motion to adjourn the debate.

Adjournment does not close the Session; nor does prorogation terminate Parliament. The former is an act which either House can perform; the latter is a power vested in the Crown, the duration of which may be subsequently shortened or extended, as the Crown pleases. All unfinished business terminates and dies with a prorogation, but during an adjournment they remain *in statu quo*, to be revised on the re-assembling of Parliament. A member who moves the adjournment of a debate, or who is in possession of the floor at the time of the adjournment, is said to be in possession of the House, with the right to re open the debate which has been interrupted. This is not the case, however, when Committees of the whole House adjourn. Prorogation never extend beyond eighty days, but it may be repeated from time to time by proclamation, and continue to be renewed until it is intended that Parliament shall meet for the despatch of business. The Crown can summon Parliament at any time by giving fourteen day's notice. Dissolution is the simple death of Parliament, and may be brought about in two ways, either by the pleasure of the Crown, or by lapse of time for which it was called into existence. There was a time when the existence of a parliament terminated by the demise of the Crown, but a special law removed this provision of the Constitution. But there is no power in the Constitution by which a Parliament in this Province can be extended beyond five years. If Parliament, at the time of the Sovereign's death, be separated by adjournment or prorogation, it must assemble immediately, or within a reasonable period. If no parliament be then in existence, the members of the last must again meet, and may serve as a parliament for six months, unless sooner prorogued.

LAW CLERKS.—It is necessary to mention these officers in particular, because the Rules of the House assign to them and the translators certain duties which must be performed, to ensure correct Legislation. It is laid down as the duty of the Law Clerk to revise all public Bills after their first reading, and to certify thereon that the same are correct; and in every subsequent stage of such Bills, the Law Clerk shall be responsible for the correctness of said Bills, should they be amended. The responsibility is increased by the fact of all Bills having to be printed in both languages, English and French, before they can be disposed of. The House is particularly fortunate in having the whole of this staff, Law Clerks and translators, most efficient.

ORDER.—By this word is meant an obedience to certain rules and regulations intended to facilitate the dispatch of business, and preserve that necessary decorum so essential in all deliberative assemblies. The Rules by which the business of Parliament is conducted are of two kinds; one class the House possesses in common with all deliberative assemblies—another is peculiar to its own existence and powers. For the proper application of all these rules, the Speaker's or Chairman's decision is had, and to this decision due deference is at all times paid. The Speaker, while in the Chair, takes no part in the debate, it being his duty to regulate the manner in which business shall be transacted: to confine those members who address the House to the subject under consideration; to give his opinion upon all things which relate to order; to put the matter in dispute into the form of a question upon which the votes of members are taken, and to declare the majority as soon as it is communicated to him by the Clerk. It is also his duty to declare the business of the House closed, and to see that the affairs of the House are correctly and properly recorded. After routine, he calls upon the member whose motion stands first on the paper of notices, or who is otherwise entitled to precedence. All motions must be seconded, or they fall to the ground; being seconded, the motion is handed in writing to the Speaker, who has to read it before debate can be had upon it—having been read, objections may be urged. There are several ways by which a motion may be opposed; it may be met by a direct negative, or by an amendment, or by a motion to postpone, or by proceeding to the next order of the day, or by moving the previous question, or by the simple motion of adjournment. A motion once read cannot be withdrawn without the permission of the House. It must not be forgotten that unless a speech is made objecting to a motion, neither mover nor seconder can speak a second time, except in explanation. If, however, a debate does arise, in which an opposition is given to the mover of a motion, he has the right of reply; but it must be understood that this privilege does not belong to the mover of an amendment. All are permitted to explain. The debate being ended, the Speaker or Chairman puts the question, and calls upon those in favor to say "Aye," and those of a contrary opinion to say "No." He then declares that in his opinion the "Ayes" or the "Noes" (as the case may be) have it. If his decision is questioned, the House divides, the "Ayes" rising and their names being taken down: the "Noes" following: the numbers are counted from the record, and declared. When an amendment has been moved, the vote is simply taken on the amendment, and then on the original question. Should the amendment be adopted, it then becomes the substantive motion, and may be amended in the same way that the original motion was amended. Thus a number of successive amendments to the original motion may be disposed of. Any member is at liberty to interrupt another by "rising to order;" which means that he rises in his place, and calls the attention of the Chair and the

House, to a breach of the orders then being committed. In debate, it is contrary to order to mention any member by name ; the same rule prevails in Committee of the Whole, except as regards the Chairman, who is called by his name, and not Mr. Chairman.

ORIGINATING BILLS.—All Bills relating to public income and expenditure, and all Bills usually called Money Bills, must originate in the Commons, and be introduced by the Government. (For fuller details see *Bills.*)

PRIVILEGES OF PARLIAMENT.—There are three kinds.
1st. The privileges which appertain to members individually.
2nd. These which belong to the House in its collective capacity.
3rd. These which belong to the House jointly.
Amongst the privileges which the Commons claim, are :—
The power of committing individuals to prison—the power of publishing matters which, if not issuing from such high authority, might become the subject of proceedings in a Court of Law,—the power of directing the Law Officers of the Crown to prosecute persons accused of offences against the laws, or affecting the privileges of Parliament,—and finally of doing anything not directly contravening an existing Act of Parliament, which may be necessary for the vindication and protection of its own rights, in the exercise of its own constitutional functions. Questions of privilege take precedence of all other proceedings, and are always in order. The privileges claimed by individual members are—freedom of speech and person, including freedom from legal arrests and seizure under process from the Courts of Law and equity. This does not extend to indictable offences or to actual contempts of the Courts of Justice. Members of Parliament are exempt from all duties, the performance of which might interfere with their prompt attendance to their Parliamentary calls. Privilege of Parliament, such as it is, continues for a convenient time after prorogation and dissolution.

ROYAL ASSENT.—The Act by which the Crown agrees to a Bill is called the Royal Assent ; this assent is usually given at the end of a Session, unless there is urgent necessity for the Act becoming Law without loss of time, in which case the Governor General, or the person administering the Government, comes down to the Upper House, and there, in the presence of both Houses, gives his assent. When this is done, either at the close of the Session or on a special occasion, the Governor General being seated on the throne, the House of Commons is summoned to the bar of the Upper House; being there, the Clerk or Clerk Assistant reads the title of the Bill, and hands it to the Chief Clerk, who says in both English and French : " In the name of Her Majesty the Queen, His Excel-" lency the Governor General sanctions this Bill," to which His Excellency manifests his assent. Bills to which the Royal assent is not given, are not noticed, but are mentioned in the "Official Gazette" as having been reserved for Her Majesty's consideration. Unless a reserve is made in the Act itself, as soon as the Royal Assent is given, the Act becomes a law, and can be proceeded on before any competent Court.

SERGEANT-AT-ARMS.—This officer, although in attendance on the House of Commons, is appointed by the Crown. It is his duty to obey the commands of the House, to apprehend and take into custody all those who are committed for any offence by the House. All the messengers and servants of the House, except the Clerks, are under his orders. He has his seat at the Bar of the House, and directs all arrangements for the maintenance of order in the approaches to, or the galleries of the House. He is of course in immediate attendance upon the Speaker, from whom he takes all orders, connected with his duties.

SESSION.—The Session is the term occupied by Parliament from its commencement to its prorogation. An adjournment does not close a Session. Parliament is annually assembled for the despatch of business. There are certain important acts which are renewed every year, and without which the Government could not be carried on, which compels the Government to meet the Representatives of the people, and render an account of the past year's transactions, once a year at least. Unless this be done, there will be no supplies. By an understanding, Parliament meets in the month of February, although circumstances sometimes arise to postpone the time. While the Crown has a right to summon Parliament where it pleases, it is generally understood that it assembles at the Seat of Government. The House being assembled, the Governor General commands the attendance of the Members of the Lower House at the Bar of the Upper House, and delivers a Speech from the Throne. This Speech is the first subject taken into consideration; no other business is commenced until the answer to it is given. As is stated elsewhere, the mere fact of one or both Houses adjourning, does not terminate the Session; it can only terminate by being prorogued by the Crown. All bills and other measures left unfinished, when the prorogation takes place, are dead, and parties who wish to revive them, must recommence their labours at the next Session, as if nothing had been done in the premises. The mere assembling of Members does not constitute a Session,—one Bill, at least, must pass both Houses, and receive the Royal Assent, before it can be called a Session.

SPEAKER.—Beyond all doubt this officer was designated Speaker, from the fact of his being the mouth piece of the Commons, in their intercourse with the Crown. He is the presiding officer of the body. He reads all communications which come from the Queen's Representative to the Commons; he has to present and read such addresses and petitions as are carried up to the Governor General by the whole House, and to deliver the usual speeches, on the part of the Commons, when presenting the Supply Bill, and other Bills, calling for particular note and remark. Through him, all witnesses and prisoners at the Bar of the House are examined, and he directs all arrangements, when the House is to be addressed by Counsel. It is his duty to deliver the reprimand of the House to any one who has incurred the penalty of receiving it; it is also his duty to issue warrants of committal, or release for breach of privilege, to communicate with any parties, when so instructed by the House. It is his duty to closely examine the provisions of private Bills so as to protect the public against any surprise, or undue encroachment or injury; to control and regulate the conduct of subordinate officers of the House; to enforce the Rules of the House; he cannot join in any debate unless in Committee of the whole House. As the presiding officer of the House, he has all the duties attached to such an office. The Speaker is chosen by the members of Parliament, subject to the approbation of the Representative of the Crown, and holds his office until the Parliament in which he is elected is dissolved. Should a member persevere in disobeying the order of the Speaker and of the House, the Speaker may "name him," as the term applies, a course uniformly followed by the censure of the House. In extreme cases, the Speaker may order members or others into custody, until the pleasure of the House be signified. On divisions, when the numbers happen to be equal, he gives the casting vote, but he never otherwise votes.

SUPPLY.—All proceedings which relate to the public income or expenditure, must originate with the Commons, and must be begun by resolution moved in Committee of Supply, which is always a Committee of the whole House. In the course of the Session, estimates are submitted to a Committee of Supply; and resolutions moved thereon, granting to the Crown the sums requisite for the management of the various departments of the Government, and the support of various public and private institutions. Such as are confirmed by the Committee of Supply are reported to the House, where they are again reconsidered and adopted, or rejected, as the case may be. Upon these a Bill is passed, and this Supply Bill furnishes the authority to the Government for disbursing the various sums appropriated. The Upper House may reject this or any other money Bill, but they cannot alter or amend the substance of a supply or money Bill; such a course would be regarded as an invasion of the Privileges of the Lower House. Before any Bill can be introduced, authorizing the expenditure of any public money, resolutions must be moved in Committee of Supply, agreed to there, reported, and confirmed by the House.

WAYS AND MEANS.—As the Committee of Supply relates to the expenditure of the country, so the functions and duties of a Committee of Ways and Means have reference to the funds by which such expenditure is to be met. Loans, duties, taxes, excise and revenue of every description, are submitted to a Committee of Ways and Means. The propositions of Government on this subject are reduced to resolutions, submitted, considered, and decided on, and such as are agreed to are reported to the House. Those which may be adopted are embodied in a Bill or Bills, and in due course and form become the Law of the land. As in Supply, the Upper House may reject these Bills, but cannot amend them; nor can the Upper House insert a pecuniary penalty in any Bill.

AREA AND BOUNDARIES

Of the Dominion of Canada, and the Provinces of Prince Edward Island and Newfoundland.

Canada, New Brunswick, Nova Scotia, Prince Edward Island and Newfoundland occupy an immense extent of territory: St. Johns, Newfoundland, the most easterly capital, being 26°. 80°. East and 9°. North of Toronto, the most westerly. It is the distance between the two being considerably over 1000 miles. These countries, however, all belong to one geographical district, which may be called the Laurentian, each claiming a portion of the shores of the Gulf of St. Lawrence, the Colonial Mediterranean.

Canada lies principally on the North side of the St. Lawrence, and the North and East sides of Lakes Ontario, Erie, Huron and Superior. In part, also, on the South side of the St. Lawrence, stretching from near Montreal to the Bay of Chaleurs. Its northerly and westerly boundaries have not been fixed. It is bounded on the South by the territories of the United States and New Brunswick. The area of Canada is given in official returns as 331, 280 square miles, being 121, 260 for Ontario, and 210,020 for Quebec.

New Brunswick is bounded by Quebec, the Gulf of St. Lawrence, Nova Scotia, the Bay of Fundy and the United States, being divided from the latter by the St. Croix River. Its area is 27,105 square miles.

Nova Scotia is a peninsula connected with New Brunswick by a low sandy itslunus. It is about 300 miles long, and about 100 miles broad at its widest. The island of Cape Breton is now a part of Nova Scotia, the Gut of Canso, which divides them, being less than a mile in breadth. The coast of Nova Scotia is everywhere indented with arms of the sea, and no part of it is more than 20 miles from salt water. Area, including Cape Breton, 18.660 squares miles.

Prince Edward Island is about 140 miles long and 34 in its greatest breadth. Its coasts are like those of Nova Scotia, much indented by bays, and no part is more than 10 miles from the sea. Unlike Nova Scotia, which has a rock-bound shore, the coast of P. E. Island is of sand or mud. Area, 2,100 square miles.

The greatest length of Newfoundland is, from North to South, 350 miles; average breadth, 130. Coast bold and rocky. Area, 40,200 square miles.

Thus the area of Canada and the two Provinces is as under :—

Canada { Ontario	121,260	square miles.
Quebec	210,020	" "
New Brunswick	27,105	" "
Nova Scotia	18,660	" "
P. E. Island	2,100	" "
Newfoundland	40,200	" "
Total	419,345	" "

If to this be added the area of Vancouver's Island, 20,000 square miles; British Columbia 200,000 square miles; and Labrador, the Hudson's Bay, and North West Territories with, say 2,750,000 square miles, we have a total for British North America of no less than 3,389,345 square miles.

The climate and productions of the Colonies are more dissimilar than might be inferred from the latitude of their settled districts. In the extreme West of Ontario, Indian Corn can be raised with profit; peaches, grapes and melons grow luxuriantly in the open air; but the district favored thus is small, and although the greater part of Canada is a magnificient region for growing all the cereals, while wheat can be raised with care in every settled part of every colony, we find by the time we travel farther Eastward than Quebec, that the people depend less and less upon the soil, until in Newfoundland they are almost exclusively concerned about the waters and buy from other countries almost all their cereal and animal food. The winter's cold varies even more than the summer's heat. Snow rarely lies more than a month in the West of Ontario. In some parts of Quebec East and the Labrador, it lies for five or six months, every season.

The diversity of the mineral resources of the several colonies is no less than that of their agricultural productions. The western peninsula of Ontario as yet alone yields petroleum; it has many valuable quarries, but few metallic ores. These, however, the shores of the upper Lakes, Central and Eastern Canada, Nova Scotia, and probably Newfoundland and New Brunswick, abundantly supply. Especially valuable are the copper mines of Canada and Newfoundland, and the gold and coal of Nova Scotia. Prince Edward Island is the worst off in this particular.

This diversity is, however, a happy thing for all the Provinces. While the general severity of their climate enforces activity among their people, the variety of their resources prevents their inhabitants from confining themselves to one branch of industry. Their wants, and the commodities with which to pay for the supply of these wants, being different, they contain within themselves the germs of a trade among themselves, which, when freed from artificial restrictions, and enabled to flow in improved channels, may some day attain vast proportions, rivalling and exceeding their already extensive commerce with foreign nations.

Supposed population of the Provinces on the 1st January 1867.

In Upper Canada	1,802,056
" Lower Canada	1,288,880
" New Brunswick	295,084
" Nova Scotia	368,781
" Prince Edward Island	91,443
" Newfoundland	130,000
Total	3,976,244

CURRENCY AND COINAGE.

CANADA.

By the Consolidated Statutes of Canada, cap. xv., the dollar is defined to be one fourth of a pound, the cent one hundred of a dollar, the mill one tenth of a cent; and it is declared that any statement as to money value may be made either in pounds, shillings and pence, or in dollars, cents and mills.

The Public Accounts have been kept in dollars and cents since 1858.

The pound currency, usually called "Halifax currency," although it is not the currency of Halifax, is "one hundred and one grains and three hundred "and twenty-one thousandths of a 'grain, Troy weight, of gold of the standard of "fineneness prescribed by law for the gold coins of the United Kingdom on the "first day of August, 1854." And "any gold coins of the standard of fineness "aforesaid which Her Majesty directs to be struck at the Royal Mint," are a legal tender in proportion to their weight.

The pound sterling (Victoria Sovereign) which contains 0.91,666 of pure gold, and weighs 123.3 grains is therefore declared equal to and legal tender for £1 4s. 4d., or $4.86⅔.

The gold Eagle of the United States coined before July 1834, is legal for $10.66⅔ or £2 13s. 4d., but if coined between that date and 1st January 1852, or as long after as the standard of fineness fixed by the laws of the United States be not changed, then only for $10.00 or £2 10s. 0d. The gold coins of the United States being "multiples or halves of the said Eagle," are legal for proportionate sums.

Other foreign gold coins may be, but have not been made legal by proclamation.

British silver coins "of the fineness fixed by law on 1st August, 1854, and "of weights bearing respectively the same proportion to the value to be assigned "to such coins in this Province which the weights of the silver coins of the "United Kingdom bore on the said day to the value assigned to them in the "United Kingdom shall, by such names as Her Majesty may assign to them in "Her Royal Proclamation, declaring them lawful money of this Province, pass "current and be a legal tender at the rates assigned to them respectively in "such proclamation." Until otherwise ordered these silver coins "shall pass "current in this Province for sums in currency equal, according to the propor- "tion hereinbefore fixed, to the sums in sterling for which they respectively "pass current in the United Kingdom."

Thus the British shilling is a legal tender for $0.24¼.

No foreign silver coin is lawful money; and British silver is only legal tender to the extent of $10.

The copper coins of the United Kingdom are a legal tender to the amount of twenty cents or one shilling currency; the penny for two cents, and subdivisions thereof in proportion.

The pence and half-pence still current in Canada where imported by the Banks. The Government has within the last few years imported both silver and and bronze coins; twenty, ten and five cent pieces of silver, and one cent pieces of bronze. The following statement shows the amount of the importation, the whole of which was taken by the Banks of the Province at par, with the exception of $4,000 in cent pieces, sold to the Province of New Brunswick.:—

CANADIAN COINAGE, FORWARDED FROM THE ROYAL MINT, LONDON :—

1858. 16th Oct..	30 Boxes Silver.	20 cent pieces.		$ 50,000 00		$ 75,000 00
		10 " "	.	10,000 00		
		5 " "	.	15,000 00		
1858. 20th Dec..	107 Boxes Silver.	20 " "	.:	96,078 40		265,738 05
		10 " "	..	111,640 20		
		5 " "	.	58,019 45		
1860. 22nd May.	485 Boxes Bronze.	1 " "		96,903 88		96,903 88
		Total..........		$ 437,641 93		$ 437,641 93

In general practice, both American quarters and British shillings are taken in shops in Canada for twenty-five cents, goods being "marked up" accordingly, and tradesmen frequently give a premium for Bank Bills.

American silver has therefore been imported in large quantities, and several million dollars worth of it are in circulation in the Province.

In Post Offices and Banks, Canadian coin is the only silver taken at its face value, the consequence of which is that almost all our silver coin is locked up in the vaults of the several Banks.

The paper money of Canada has been until of late exclusively issued by the Banks, and is of the denominations of $1, $2, $4, $5, $10, $20, $50, $100.

NEW BRUNSWICK.

The New Brunswick legal dollar is the same as that of Canada, bearing the same relation to the English sovereign. The Bank notes are of denominations as low as $1, and are considered equal to gold.

The coins imported by the Province are of the same denominations as those of Canada ; viz: 20, 10 and 5 cent pieces, of silver, and one cent of bronze. The Government made two importations—the first of $30,011.00 in shillings ; $15,012.90 in six pences ; $5,002.75 in three pences, and $3,000.00 in cents. The second was of $44,985 35 in silver coins in about the same proportion, and of $9,980.87 in copper. Total face value $107,992.87, total cost £9,872 17s. 11d. sterling.

These coins are now the common metallic currency of the Province, the American silver quarter being taken for 20 cents only, and the British shilling being legal only as 24 cents, which is below their intrinsic value, and therefore drives them out of circulation.

NOVA SCOTIA.

The sovereign of the United Kingdom is equal to five dollars in the currency of Nova Scotia. The doubloon, if not less weight than 415 grains and containing not less than 360 grains of pure gold is $16.

The Peruvian, Mexican, Columbian and old Spanish dollars, of the full weight of 416 grains and containing not less than 373 grains of pure silver are legal for 4s. 2d. sterling or $1.04. The silver coins of the United Kingdom are legal tender, to the extent of $10, at the following rates :

The Crown, $1.25 ; the half Crown, $0 62½; the florin, $0.50 ; the shilling, $0.25 ; the six pence, $0.12½ ; the four pence, $0.08.

No other silver coin is legal tender, but the American "quarter" passes current at 22½ cents.

The copper coin of the Province is the only legal tender in copper, and then only to the extent of 25 cents.

All Public Accounts are kept and all judgments must be entered and executions taken out in dollars and cents.

The Province has issued no silver coins. It has called in its old issue of pence and half pence, and substituted an issue of bronze cents and half cents to the face value of $17,903, of which about $2,000 is in half cents

The Statutes declare that " any person issuing as circulating currency any " promissory note or bank note or bill for a less sum than $20 shall for every " such offence forfeit forty dollars." Banks are therefore debarred from issuing small notes, and the Treasury notes, which are of the denominations of $4 and $5, are in demand. Their amount in circulation at the end of June, 1866, was $502.488. They are not a legal tender, except for duties, while on the other hand the Receiver General is authorized to pay warrants with them. They are not, however, at a discount, for if the Banks were not to receive them, the Government would do so and give the parties presenting them a cheque on the Bank of Nova Scotia, payable in gold.

PRINCE EDWARD ISLAND.

The currency of Prince Edward Island is more complex than that of any of the other North American Colonies.

By 12 Victoria, chapter 24, the British sovereign is a legal tender at thirty shillings island currency, and British silver in proportion.

The American Eagle ($10) is legal at £3 currency, aliquot parts in proportion.

British gold is therefore more abundant in the Island than American.

The gold doubloon of not less than 415 grains is legal at £4 16s.

The United States, Peruvian, Chilian and Spanish milled dollars and the dollar of Central America being of not less weight than 412 grains are legal at 6s. 3d. Island currency, and aliquot parts in proportion.

The French five franc piece is legal at 5s. 6.; and its subdivisions at the same rate.

Copper coins legally current in the United Kingdom, Canada and New Brunswick are legal in Prince Edward Island, penny for penny. But a British half penny is not legal for more than a half penny, though worth nearly as much as an Island penny.

The Public Accounts are kept partly in Island currency, partly in sterling.

The Prince Edward Island Government has coined no money, unless we take into account its Treasury bills of 5s. and multiples. The Banks have issued a few copper coins.

NEWFOUNDLAND.

The British Sovereign, legal tender for........ $4.80 currency.
The Gold Eagle (U. S.) "   "   " .... 9.85 "
The Silver Coins of the United Kingdom legal tender for sums in currency proportionately to gold coins.
The Doubloon, legal tender for............. $15.35 currency.
The American, Peruvian, Mexican, Columbian
and old Spanish Dollar, legal tender for.. 100 cents.
Provided that no tender in silver to a greater amount than Ten Dollars shall be valid.

ISLAND COINAGE.

Two dollar gold pieces $20,000
Silver 20 cent pieces....................... 20,000
"   "   " 8,000
"   "   " 4,000
Bronze Cents............................... 2,400

CURRENCY TABLE.

Canadian Currency.			Sterling.		Canadian Currency.			Sterling.		Canadian Currency.				Sterling.		
c.	s.	d.	s.	d.	c.	s.	d.	s.	d.	$ c.	£	s.	d.	£	s.	d.
1		½		½	32	1	7½	1	3¾	63		3	1¾		2	7
2		1¼		1	33	1	7¾	1	4¼	64		3	2½		2	7½
3		1¾		1½	34	1	8½	1	4¾	65		3	3		2	8
4		2½		2	35	1	9	1	5¼	66		3	3½		2	8½
5		3		2½	36	1	9½	1	5¾	67		3	4½		2	9
6		3½		3	37	1	10¼	1	6¼	68		3	4¾		2	9½
7		4¼		3½	38	1	10¾	1	6¾	69		3	5½		2	10
8		4¾		4	39	1	11½	1	7¼	70		3	6		2	10½
9		5½		4½	40	2	0	1	7¾	61		3	6½		2	11
10		6		5	41	2	0½	1	8¼	72		3	7¼		2	11½
11		6½		5½	42	2	1¼	1	8¾	73		3	7¾		3	0
12		7¼		6	43	2	1¾	1	9¼	74		3	8½		3	0½
13		7¾		6½	44	2	2¼	1	9¾	75		3	9		3	1
14		8½		7	45	2	3	1	10½	76		3	9½		3	1½
15		9		7½	46	2	3½	1	10¾	77		3	10¼		3	2
16		9½		8	47	2	4¼	1	11¼	78		3	10¾		3	2½
17		10¼		8½	48	2	4¾	1	11¾	79		3	11½		3	3
18		10¾		9	49	2	5½	2	0¼	80		4	0		3	3½
19		11¾		9¼	50	2	6	2	0¾	81		4	0½		3	4
20	1	0		9¾	51	2	6½	2	1¼	82		4	1¼		3	4½
21	1	0½		10¼	52	2	7¼	2	1¾	83		4	1¾		3	5
22	1	1¼		10¾	53	2	7¾	2	2¼	84		4	2½		3	5½
23	1	1¾		11¼	54	2	8½	2	2¾	85		4	3		3	6
24	1	2½		11¾	55	2	9	2	3	86		4	3½		3	6½
25	1	3	1	0¼	56	2	9½	2	3½	87		4	4½		3	7
26	1	3½	1	0¾	57	2	10½	2	4	88		4	4¾		3	7½
27	1	4½	1	1¼	58	2	10¾	2	4½	89		4	5½		3	8
28	1	4¾	1	1¾	59	2	11½	2	5	90		4	6		3	8¼
29	1	5½	1	2¼	60	3	0	2	5½	1.00		5	0		4	1¼
30	1	6	1	2¾	61	3	0½	2	6	5.00	1	5	0	1	0	0½
31	1	6½	1	3¼	62	3	1¼	2	6½	10.00	2	10	0	2	1	1¼

To Convert Pence into Cents.—Add a cypher to any number of pence and divide by 6. Example: To 44 pence, add a cypher, 440; which, divided by 6, gives 73 2-6ths, say 73 cents.

To Convert Cents into Pence.—Multiply any number of cts. by 6, and put off the last figure, which is tenths. Example: 73 cents, multiplied by 6, gives 438, or 43 pence and 8-10ths, say 44d.

To Convert Sterling into Currency.—To the given sum, add one-fifth of itself and one-twelfth of that one-fifth.

Currency into Sterling.—Multiply by 60 and divide by 73.

GAME AND FISHERY LAWS.

CANADA.

In Ontario, the close season for Deer or Fawn, Elk, Moose or Caribou begins on the 1st January, and ends on the 1st September. They are not allowed to be trapped or taken by any traps or snares whatever. The close season for Wild Turkey, Grouse, Partridge or Pheasant, is between the 1st February and the 1st September; Quail between the 1st February and the 1st October; Woodcock, 1st March and 15th July; and Wild Swan, Goose, Duck, Widgeon or Teal, 1st April and 1st August. Beaver, Muskrat, Mink, Sable, Otter, or Fisher, shall not be trapped or killed between the 1st May and the 1st November.

It is unlawful to fish for, catch, buy or sell the following fish in Ontario between the dates named:—Speckled Trout, 20th September and 1st April; White Fish, in any way, between 19th Nov. and 1st December, and by net between 30th May and 1st August. (The close season for Bass, Pike, Pickerel (*dorée*), and Maskinongé, is regulated by Order in Council, to suit different localities.)

The close season for Red or Grey Deer, Moose, Elk, Reindeer and Caribou in Quebec, is from 1st February to 1st September; for Woodcock or Snipe, 1st March to 1st August; Grouse, Partridge, Ptarmigan, or Pheasant, 1st March to 20th August; Wild Swan, Wild Goose or Wild Duck of the kinds known as Mallard, Gray Duck, Black Duck, Wood Duck, Teal, Widgeon, or any other kind of Wild Duck, 20th May to 20th August; Muskrat, 10th May to 1st March.

It is also unlawful to fish for, catch, buy or sell any of the following fish between the dates named, in Quebec:—Salmon, 31st July and 1st May, (fly surface fishing is, however, permitted between 30th April and 31st August.) Trout or "Lunge," 15th September and 15th December; Bass and Pickerel (*dorée*), Pike and Maskinongé, 30th April and 1st June.

It is unlawful to kill or snare any birds whatsoever, excepting Eagles, Falcons, Hawks, Wild Pigeons, Kingfishers, Crows or Ravens, between the 1st of March and the 1st of August in each year. This was added to the Game Law for the purpose of protecting the insectivorous birds, and has already proved beneficious by greatly increasing their number.

The Fish and Game Clubs annually make valuable reports on the condition, &c., of the Fish and Game, and offer additional rewards from their own funds for the conviction of offenders against the provisions of the law.

NEW BRUNSWICK.

In New Brunswick no moose shall be killed between the 1st February and 1st May—penalty $40,00; no herrings taken in their spawning grounds in the Bay of Fundy between 15th July and 15th October—penalty $20,00; no salmon taken in nets later than August 31st, or by the rod later than September 15th, or at any time between Saturday's sunset and Monday's sunrise.

NOVA SCOTIA.

The Revised Statutes of Nova Scotia (Cap. 92,) provides that no person shall kill any partridge, snipe or woodcock between 1st March and 1st September under a penalty of $2 for each offence. No one shall kill any moose or cariboo between 15th February and 1st September, nor a cow-moose between 1st January and 1st September. The flesh must be carried out of the woods within three days if in September or October, and fourteen in the other lawful months. No one person may kill more than five moose or cariboo in one season, nor shall any hunting party kill more than five at one hunt. No one is allowed to kill pheasants. No one may kill the otter, mink or muskrat between 1st May and 1st November—penalty $8,00. It is altogether forbidden to kill the smaller kinds of birds: robins, swallows, sparrows, &c., and birds of song—penalty $1,00 for each bird killed.

Chapter 95 provides that no salmon shall be taken in any river west of Halifax between 31st July and 1st March, nor in any river running into the Bay of Fundy or east of Halifax between 15th August and 1st March, nor in salt water later than October 20—penalty $40. There are no laws respecting trout.

B. N. A. Year Book, 1867.

STAMP DUTIES.

CANADA.

On Bills of Exchange, Drafts and Promissory Notes.

In computing the duty, it must be borne in mind that any interest payable at maturity with the principal, is to be counted as part of the amount.

AMOUNT.	Singly.	Duplicate each part.	Triplicate each part.
$25 and under..............	$0.01	$0.01	$0.01
Over 25 and not exceeding $ 50..	0.02	0.01	0.01
" 50 " " 100..	0.03	0.02	0.01
" 100 " " 200..	0.06	0.04	0.02
" 200 " " 300..	0.09	0.06	0.03
" 300 " " 400..	0.12	0.08	0.04
" 400 " " 500..	0.15	0.10	0.05
" 500 " " 600..	0.18	0.12	0.06

EXTRACT FROM ACT OF 1865.—"The person affixing such adhesive stamp, shall, at the time of affixing the same, write or stamp thereon the date at which it is affixed, and such stamp shall be held *primâ facie* to have been affixed at the date stamped or written thereon, and if no date be so stamped or written thereon, such adhesive stamp shall be of no avail ; any person willfully writing or stamping a false date on any adhesive stamp shall incur a penalty of one hundred dollars for each such offence."

FOREIGN MAILS.

Table exhibiting the rates to the principal counties in postal communication with Canada.

DESTINATION.	Letters.	Papers.	DESTINATION.	Letters.	Papers.
	Cts.	Cts.		Cts.	Cts.
Australia..	23	5	Hamburgh..............	23	6
Austria.	23	6	Holland	17	3
*Bermuda	23	3	Norway.................	27	6
*British West Indies.......	23	3	*Nova Scotia.............	5	1
**British Columbia	10	2	*Newfoundland *viâ* Boston..	12½	3
Belgium	19	5	Portugal, ¼ oz............	19	3
Bremen	23	6	Prussia	23	6
*Cuba....................	20	3	Russia...................	31	6
California................	10	1	*Red River	10	1
Denmark.................	29	6	Spain, ¼ oz..............	23	6
France, ¼ oz.............	17	5	Sweden.................	23	6
Gibraltar	23	3	*Vancouver..............	10	2

* All of these to be addressed "*viâ* United States."

** To San Francisco only, an additional charge on delivery.

N. B.—With the exception of those marked with an asterisk, all are to be sent by *Canadian Line* only ; for Cunard Line, add to the above rates 5 cents for letters.

TABLE OF DISTANCES

FROM OTTAWA TO THE PRINCIPAL CITIES AND TOWNS IN CANADA.

BY RAILWAY.	Miles.	BY RAILWAY AND STEAMER.	Miles.
Going East from Ottawa.		BY THE OTTAWA RIVER AND ST. LAW-RENCE NAVIGATION.	
To Prescott Junction...........	54		
Thence to Montreal............	112	Ottawa to Grenville.............	63
" " St. Hyacinthe.......	35	Thence to Carrillon	13
" " Richmond..........	41	" " Lachine..............	43
" " Quebec.............	96	" " Montreal.	9
" " L'Islet.............	60	" " Sorel................	45
" " Rivière du Loup*....	65	" " Three Rivers..........	48
Arthabaska to Three Rivers......	35	" " Quebec..............	87
Montreal to Sherbrooke........	101	" " Murray Bay..........	76
" " Portland...........	297	" " Tadousac............	44
" " Rouse's Point......	49		

* From Rivière du Loup there is a Tri-Weekly Stage to Grand Falls and Woodstock, connecting the lat er place with the Railway at St. John's and all places in New Brunswick and Nova Scotia.

		Going West from Ottawa.	
Quebec to Halifax viâ *the Temiscouata Road, Woodstock, Fredericton, St. John and Amherst.*		To Prescott Junction..........	54
		Thence to Brockville..........	13
		" " Kingston...........	47
Quebec, by rail to R. du Loup...	128	" " Belleville..........	50
Province Line...............	67	" " Cobourg	41
New Brunswick—		" " Port Hope..........	7
Little Falls.................	12	" " Toronto............	63
Grand Falls.................	38	" " Stratford...........	88
River de Chute.............	33	" " Sarnia.............	80
Woodstock..................	40	" " Detroit.............	100
Fredericton	63	Port Hope to Lindsay..........	43
St. John, by rail.............	66	" " Peterboro........	31
Petitcodiac.................	90	London to Port Stanley.........	24
Nova Scotia—Amherst.........	44	Toronto to Collingwood.........	94
Truro......................	63	" " Hamilton	39
Halifax.....................	61	Suspension Bridge to Windsor...	229
		Brockville to Sand Point.......	74
		Smith's Fall to Perth..........	12

The international Company's Steamers run from Boston, and Portland to St. John N. B.

Leave Boston and Portland every Monday and Thursday.

Leave St. Johns, N. B. every Monday and Thursday.

THE POST OFFICE—OTTAWA.

Office hours—8 a. m. to 7 p. m.

DELIVERING AND CLOSING OF MAILS.

MAILS.	DELIVERED.	CLOSED.
Eastern, Montreal, Quebec, &c.	11.40 a. m. and 6.00 p. m.	1.00 p. m.
Western, Toronto, Hamilton	11.40 a. m.	7.20 a. m. and 1.00 p. m.
United States.	11.40 a. m. and 6.00 p. m.	7.20 a. m.
Aylmer, and offices above, on North side of the Ottawa.	8.00 a. m. and 11.30 a. m.	11.30 a. m. and 5.50 p. m.
Arnprior, Sand Point, Renfrew, Pembroke & Offices on S. side of the Ottawa.	6.00 p. m.	8.30 a. m.
Bell's Corners, Richmond, Perth, &c.	5.30 p. m.	8.00 p. m.
Buckingham, L'Orignal, Grenville, and Lower Ottawa, by Stage.	8.00 a. m.	6.00 p. m.
Kemptville, Osgoode, & Line of Ottawa and Prescott Railway.	6.00 p. m.	7.20 a. m.
Chelsea, Wakefield, and Upper Gatineau.	5.30 p. m.	8.00 p. m.
Templeton and East Templeton.	12.30 a. m.	m.

BRITISH MAILS.

British Mails close per Canadian steamer from Portland, every Thursday at 9 p. m.; per Cunard steamer every Saturday at 12.30 p. m. A supplementary mail per Canadian steamer will be closed at 12 noon every Friday.

Money Orders on Money Order Offices in Canada, Great Britain and Ireland, New Brunswick, Nova Scotia, Newfoundland, and Prince Edward Island can be obtained at this office. Also Postage and Bill Stamps.

Letters for New Brunswick, Nova Scotia, and P. E. Island, *via* Portland, should be mailed before 1 p. m. on Wednesday and Saturday; and Newfoundland, *via* Boston, before the close of each Cunard steamer's mail from that port.

BANK AGENCIES.

Bank of British North America. A. C. Kelty, manager. Office: 140, Wellington, street.

Bank of Montreal. A. Drummond, manager. Office: 202, Wellington street.

Quebec Bank. H. V. Noel, manager. Office: Wellington street.

Ontario Bank. W. Wade, manager. Office: Corner of Sparks and Metcalf street.

Royal Canadian Bank. W. P. Hayes, manager. Office: Desbarats' Block, Sparks Street.

MONTREAL TELEGRAPH COMPANY.

Main office, Metcalf street. Branch offices, Parliament Buildings and Russell House. Office hours 8 a. m. to 8 p. m.

CROWN TIMBER.

A. J. Russell, Agent, and Inspector of Crown Timber Agencies of Canada; Office, corner Hugh and Queen Streets.

RIDEAU CANAL.

James D. Slater, superintendent; Office, 126 Wellington Street.

BOARD OF TRADE.

Hon. Jas. Skead, president; G. II. Perry, Secretary.

CUSTOM HOUSE.

Office, Elgin Street.—Duncan Graham, collector; Office hours from 10 a.m. to 3 p.m.

ASSOCIATION OF LUMBER MANUFACTURERS.

Allan Gilmour, president; Richard McConnell, vice-president; David Moore, Joseph Aumond, Levi Young, Hon. James Skead, and Robert Conroy, directors; Robert Skead, treasurer; G. H. Perry, secretary; Hon. James Skead, David Moore, and the Secretary, audit committee.

GAS COMPANY.

D. W. Coward, Secretary-treasurer. The Works are situated on King Street, between Rideau and York ; James Perry, manager.

OTTAWA AND PRESCOTT RAILWAY.

General Offices, Desbarats' Building, Spark Street, Ottawa. Superintendent's Office at Railway Station Prescott. Length of road 54 miles. Thomas Reynolds, managing director; T. S. Detlor, Superintendent.

BUILDING SOCIETIES.

Ottawa Permanent Building Society.—Regular meetings, second Thursday of every month. William Hay, secretary and treasurer. Office, No. 19 Sparks Street.

Ottawa Union Building Society.—Geo. N. Burke, secretary and treasurer.

Civil Service Building and Savings Society.—President, John Langton, M.A., auditor; vice-president, W. H. Griffin, deputy postmaster general; Directors, E. A. Meredith, LL.D., assistant secretary, West; G. E. Desbarats; J. F. Taylor, clerk of the Senate; John Ashworth, cashier, post office department; Alfred Todd, chief clerk, private bill office, House of Commons; secretary and treasurer, Arthur Harvey, audit office; solicitor, II. Bernard, crown law department; Bankers, the Bank of Montreal.

LITERARY SOCIETIES.

French Canadian Institute.—(Organized 1848.—Meets in their own Hall, opposite Notre Dame Cathedral, every Thursday evening. The library and reading-room open from 9 A.M. to 10 P.M. The library contains 1000 volumes. Joseph Tassé, secretary.

St. Patrick's Literary Association.—The Society meets every Tuesday evening, in the St. Patrick's Hall, Sussex street, opposite Notre Dame Cathedral. The library and reading-room are open every evening from 7 to 10.

Mechanics' Institute and Athenæum.—Library and reading-room, Sparks street, W. P. Lett, corresponding secretary.

Ottawa Natural History Society.—Sparks street, Dr. Van Courtland, curator.

Ottawa Literary Association.—Meets every Wednesday evening, in McCarthy's Hall, Central Town.

OTTAWA VOLUNTEER MILITIA.

Commandant: Lt. Colonel Thos. Wily. March 16,66.

Field Battery.
Septr. 27,55

Captain:
Jas. Forsyth, D. I.   Septr. 28,66
1st Lieutenants:
George Clarke,   April   5,67
Campbell Macnab.   May   17,61
2nd Lieutenant:
Jno. Stewart.   May   3,67
Paymaster:
Alex. S. Woodburn.   May   3,67
Surgeon:
Ed. Van Cortland.   Novr. 14,55

Provisional Brigade.
Augt. 10,66

Major Commanding:
Alfred G. Forrest.   March 15,66

No. 1 Battery.
March 22,61

Captain:
A. Parsons.   Novr. 30,66
1st Lieutenant:
W. G. Bedard.   March 8,67
2nd Lieutenant:
Jno. A. Gemmill.   June   7,67

No. 2 Battery.
March 16,66

Captain:
Thos. Ross, M.   March 17,65
1st Lieutenant:
Henry E. Steele.   June   8,66
2nd Lieutenant:
W. H. Cotton.   March 23,66

No. 3 Battery.
June   8,66

Captain:
Chs. E. Perry.   June 15,66
1st Lieutenant:
Alex. Lord Russell.   Augt. 31,66
2nd Lieutenant:
Frs. C. Clemow.   Septr. 14,66

No. 4 Battery.
Augt. 10,66

Captain:
Jas. Adams.   Augt. 10,66

1st Lieutenant:
Archd. Graham.   Septr. 14,66
2nd Lieutenant:
Wm. H. Cluff,   Feby. 22,67
Paymaster:
Chs. E. Brush.   Decr. 14,66

Provisional Battalion.
Octr.   5,66

Head Quarters, Ottawa.

Major Commanding:
Donald M. Grant.   Decr. 21,66

No. 1 Coy., Ottawa.
April   3,56

Captain:
Michael J. May   Decr. 21,66
Lieutenant:
Danl. Mowatt.   "
Ensign:
A. Mathewman   "

No. 2 Coy. Ottawa.
June 19,61

Captain:
Griffidus Mann.   March 8,67
Lieutenant:
E. K. McGillivray.   "
Ensign:
Wm. Cherry.   "

No. 4 Coy. Wakefield.
Septr. 28,66

Captain:

Lieutenant:
Cyrus Ashford.   "
Ensign:
Adoniram Cates.   "
Paymaster:
R. E. O'Connor.   Decr. 21,66
Adjutant:
Jas. P. McPherson.   "
Quarter Master:
Robt. Lang.   Novr. 8,67
Surgeon:
Joseph Garvey, M. D.   { April 17,56 / Decr. 21,66

OTTAWA VOLUNTEER MILITIA.—*Continued.*

The "Civil Service Rifle Regiment."		Brinsley King,	May 23,67
	Septr. 21,66	John Walsh,	July 12,67
Lieutenant Colonel :		Ensigns :	
Thomas Wily.	Septr. 21,66	Charles Bossé,	Septr. 21,66
		C. Herbert O'Meara,	Novr. 16,66
Majors :		George Hy. Lane,	Feby. 15,67
Hewitt Bernard, *l.c.*	"	Toussaint Trudeau,	June 21,67
Chs. J. Anderson.	"	Wm. B. Ross,	"
Captains :		G. E. M. Sherwood.	Octr. 11,67
R. S. M. Bouchette,	"	Paymaster :	
Jno. Langton,	"	Horace Wicksteed.	Septr. 21,66
Wm. B. Lindsay,	"		
Geo. E Desbarats,	"	Adjutant and Captain :	
Wm. White,	"	John Le Breton Ross.	Feby. 8,67
Fredk. Braun.	July 26,67	Quarter Master :	
Lieutenants :		John Ashworth.	Septr. 21,66
H. C. Hay,	Septr. 21,66	Surgeon :	
E. T. Taché,	"	Wm. Wilson, M. D.	{ Decr. 10,61
J. Cunningham Stewart,	"		{ Novr. 16.66
Jno. Le Breton Ross,	Novr. 9,66		
Henry R. Smith,	Feby. 8, 67	6 *Companies.*	

CHURCHES.

Christ Church, (Church of England) Sparks street. Hours of service, 11 a. m., 3½ p. m. and 7 p. m.

Notre Dame Cathedral, (Roman Catholic,) Sussex street. Hours of service, 6, 8 and 10 a. m. and 7 p. m. from Easter to St. Michael's Day, 6, 8 and 10 a. m. and 6 p. m. from St. Michael until Easter.

St. Joseph Church, (Roman Catholic), Sandy Hill. Hours of service 8 and 10 a. m., and 7 p. m.

St. Andrew's Church, (Roman Catholic). Sparks Street. Hours of service, 8 and 10 a. m., and 7 p. m.

Chapel of Ease, (Church of England), Sussex street. Hours of service, 11 a. m. and 6 p. m.

St. Alban's, (Church of England), Daly street. Hours of service, 11 a. m. and 4 p. m.

St. Andrew's (Church of Scotland), Wellington street. Hours of service 11 a. m. and 6½ p. m.

Knox's Free Church, Daly street. Hours of service, 11 a. m. and 6½ p. m.

Free Church, Bank street. Hours of service, 11 a. m. and 6½ p. m.

Congregational, Corner of Albert and Elgin streets. Hours of service, 11 a. m. and 6½ p. m.

Wesleyan Methodist Church, Metcalf, corner of Queen's street. Hours of service, 10½ a. m. and 6½ p. m.

Methodist Episcopal Church, Corner of York and Dalhousie streets. Hours of service, 11½ a. m. and 6½ p. m.

Methodist Episcopal Church, Corner of Queen and Bridge streets, le Breton's Flat. Hours of service, 10½ a. m. and 6½ p. m.

Baptist Church, Queen's streets. Hours of service, 11 a. m. and 6½ p. m.

NEWSPAPERS.

The Canada Gazette. G. E. Desbarats, publisher. Office : Desbarats' Block, corner of Sparks and O'Connor streets.

The Ottawa Citizen. (Daily $6, Weekly $1, per annum,) office : 20½, Rideau street.

The Ottawa Times. (Daily $5, Weekly $1,) per annum,) office : 56, Sparks street.

The Daily News. ($4 per annum,) office : St. Paul street.

Le Canada. (Tri-weekly, $4,) office : 26, York street.

The Volunteer Review. (Weekly, $2 per annum,) office : Rideau street.

THE CITY CABS.

TARIFF OF CHARGES FOR LICENSED CARRIAGES FOR THE CONVEYANCE OF PASSENGERS, WITHIN THE LIMITS OF THE CITY OF OTTAWA.

Carriages drawn by two horses.

	Cts.
For the conveyance of not exceeding Four Passengers, hired by the Hour—1st Hour	75
Each subsequent Hour	37½

Carriages drawn by one horse.

	Cts.
Not exceeding three Passengers—1st Hour	50
Each subsequent Hour	30

Each passenger shall be allowed a reasonable amount of Luggage.

	Cts.
For the conveyance of one Passenger from the Steamboat Landing, or Railway Terminus, to any part of Upper Town, East of Pooley's Bridge	25
West of Pooley's Bridge	37½
Each Additional Passenger	12½
One Passenger from Steamboat Landing or Railway Terminus to any place in Lower Town	20
Each Additional Passenger	12½
One Passenger from any of the Carters Stands in Lower Town to any part in the Upper Town, East of Pooley's Bridge, and returning, and *vice versâ,* provided the time in waiting does not exceed 15 minutes	12½

	Cts.
West of Pooley's Bridge and Returning	25
Each Additional Passenger	12½
One Passenger from the Eastern to the Western limits of the City of Ottawa, or from the Northern to the Southern limits of same, and returning, and *vice versâ*	37½
Without Returning	25
Each Additional Passenger	12½
One Passenger from any part of Upper Town East of Pooley's Bridge to Steamboat Landing or Railway Terminus and Returning, provided the time in waiting does not exceed half an hour	25
Each Additional Passenger	12½
One Passenger from any part of Upper Town, West of Pooley's Bridge to Steamboat Landing or Railway Terminus, and Returning provided the time in waiting does not exceed half an hour	37½
Each Additional Passenger	12½

Certified,

WILLIAM P. LETT,
City Clerk.

N. B.—" Any Licensed Carter who shall refuse to exhibit his Tariff of Fees, when demanded, shall forfeit all claims to payment for the service then rendered."

Advertisers who will continue their advertisement in the 2nd Edition of the "Hand Book" will be entitled to a Discount of 25 per cent. for that Edition.

DRUGGISTS.

EDMOND GIROUX, Chemist & Druggist, Dealer in Patent Medicines, Perfumery, Combs, Brushes, Druggists Fancy Goods, &c., Garden, Grass and Flower Seeds, St. Peter Street, Quebec.

J. B. MARTEL, Chemist & Druggist, St. John Street, without, Quebec.

R. DUGAL, Druggist, Jacques Cartier Market Square, Crown Street, St. Roch, Quebec.

O L. GIROUX, M. D., Druggist, 49, St. Peter Street, Lower Town, Quebec.

DRY GOODS.

A. HAMEL & FRÈRES, Importers of English, French, American & German Goods. Wholesale, 14, Mountain St., Retail, 22, Sous-le-Fort Street, Quebec. { A. HAMEL, JOS. HAMEL, F. E. HAMEL.

THIBAUDEAU, THOMAS & CO., Wholesale Importers of Staple and Fancy Dry Goods, corner St. Peter and Sous-le-Fort Streets, Quebec.

TETU & GARNEAU, Importers of British and Foreign Dry Goods, Wholesale only, No. 45, St. Peter Street, Quebec. { C. TETU, P. GARNEAU.

HATTER.

A. LAPOINTE & SON, No. 9½, Fabrique Street, Upper Town, the only Hat Manufacturers in Quebec.

GILDERS.

A LMERAS & BELANGER, Gilders No. 9, St. John Street, St. John Suburb, Quebec. Constantly on hand an assortment of Mouldings for Pictures or Looking-Glass Frames, &c., &c., at the lowest price.

GROCERS.

J. A. MAILLOUX, Grocer, 38, Crown Street, St. Roch, Quebec. Wholesale and Retail Merchant of Tea, Sugar, Wines, Liquors, &c., &c., at very reduced prices.

DION & DUBEAU, Wholesale and Retail Merchants of Wines, Liquors, Groceries, &c., &c., No. 28, Crown Street, St. Roch, Quebec.

FLOUR MERCHANTS.

EDWARD MATTE & CO., Flour Merchants, St. Andrews Wharf, Lower Town, Quebec. E. M. & Co., keep constantly on hand, an extensive Stock of Corn, Peas, Bran, Oats, Gaudriole, &c., &c.

T THÉBERGE, Flour and Grain Merchant Champlain Market, Quebec. The highest price is paid for Linseed.

HARDWARES.

N. LEMIEUX & NOEL, (to the Sign of the Smith Vice), Importers of Hardware, 60, St. Peter Street, Lower Town, Quebec.
N. B.—House furnishing, glasses, paints, oils, turpentine, brushes, glue, nails, spikes, shovels and spades, sheetiron, tin, stoves, chains, steel, axes, &c., &c.

F. N. GINGRAS, Sign of the Golden Key, Importer of Hardware and Cutlery, No. 46, St. Peter Street, Lower Town, Quebec, has constantly on hand, bar Iron, Steel, Paints, dry and in Oil, Varnish, Turpentine, Linseed Oil, Window Glasses, Putty, &c., &c.

BOWLING SALOON.

BOWLING SALOON, kept by G. MERCIER & Co., No. 17, Palace Street, Quebec. Will constantly keep on hand an assortment of the best Wines, Liquors, Cigars, &c.

NEWSPAPERS.

LE CANADIEN, a Political, Commercial and Literary Journal, founded in 1808. Editor & Proprietor, Honble. FRANÇOIS EVANTUREL, Quebec.

LE JOURNAL DE QUÉBEC, Political, Commercial and Literary Journal. Proprietor & Publisher, A. COTÉ, Quebec.

THE MORNING CHRONICLE, Proprietor and Editor, J. J. FOOTE, Quebec. Daily Edition, per annum, $6, Daily Edition, for the Session, $2, Weekly Edition, per annum, $2.

L'ÉVÉNEMENT, French daily Paper. Editor and Proprietor, HECTOR FABRE, Quebec. Daily $5—Tri-weekly $3.—Weekly $2.

COURRIER DU CANADA, Editor & Proprietor, LÉGER BROUSSEAU, Printer and Stationer, Quebec.

WATCHMAKERS.

S. BEDARD, Watchmaker and Jeweller, 37, St. John Street, Upper Town, Quebec.

M. LAMONTAGNE, Importer of Watches, Jewellery, Spectacles, &c., &c., of every descriptions, No. 71, St. John Street, foot of Fabrique, Quebec. Clocks, Watches, Jewellery and Spectacles neatly repaired and warranted.

HECTOR DROLET, manufacturing Jeweller, St. John Street, No. 12, Quebec.

CYRILLE DUQUET, Clockmaker, No. 1, Fabrique Street, Quebec.

JOSEPH DONATI, Watchmaker and Jeweller, St. John Street, No. 8½, Quebec.

CONTRACTOR.

J. BTE. BERTRAND & Co., Contractors, 29½, Richardson Street, St. Roch, Quebec.

TINSMITH.

L. J. MERCIER, Tinsmith and Founder, will execute all work in his line, at No. 37, Paul Street, Lower Town, Quebec.

SHOEMAKERS.

SILLA COTÉ, Boot and Shoemaker, No. 24, Couillard Street, Upper Town, Quebec. Boots and Shoes of the first quality and latest style for Ladies, Gents and Children, sold at moderate prices.

CHARLES BOIVIN, Boot and Shoemaker, St. John Street, St. John's Suburb, No. 51, Quebec.

MEDALS and Diplomas obtained at the Exhibitions of London, New York and France. JOSEPH BARBEAU, Boot and Shoemaker, 72, St. John Street, St. John's Suburb, Quebec. All sorts of Gaiters, &c.

J. BTE. RICHARD, Manufacturer and Wholesale Merchant of Boots and Shoes, No. 41, St. John Street, without, has constantly on hand a varied assortment of the best Boots and Shoes, which he will offer for sale at moderate prices.

STATIONER.

M. L. CRÉMAZIE, No. 12, Buade Street, Quebec. Books of Literature, Science, Arts, &c., Office Requisites of all kinds, Fancy articles, &c.

HOTELS.

UNION HOTEL, 53. St. Peter Street, Quebec. S. CARRIER, Proprietor.

RESTAURANT.—L. A. BOISVERT, 47, St. Peter Street, Quebec.

MOUNTAIN HILL HOUSE, 5, Mountain Street, Quebec. Meals at all hours.   E. C. FRECHETTE.

ST. GEORGE RESTAURANT, GEO. BELLEAU, Du Fort Street, Upper Town, Quebec.

PAUL COUTURE,

BOOT AND SHOE MANUFACTURER,

37, ST. JOHN STREET (without),

QUEBEC.

ECONOMY. SOLIDITY, ELEGANCE,

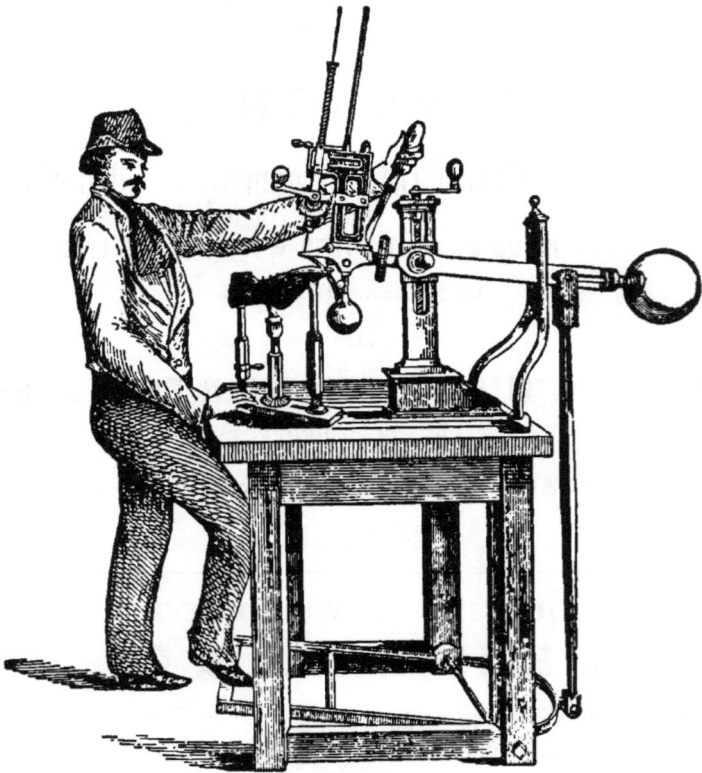

MULTIPLE MANUFACTURE.

NEW MACHINE FOR SCREWING SHOES.

At his voyage to Paris, in June last, Mr. P. Couture made the acquisition of two machines, which are now in operation in his workshop. The Boots and Shoes manufactured there are faultless. Mr. Couture is the only one in Canada who possesses this kind of machine.

GARANT & TRUDEL,

(LATE HARDY),

STATIONERS,

OPPOSITE THE BARRACKS, UPPER TOWN,

No. 12, FABRIQUE STREET,

QUEBEC.

Import several articles from England, France, Germany and the Continent, such as Books, China Ware, Perfumery, Church Ornaments, Bells, Mass Wine, Wax Tapers, &c. They will punctually execute all orders committed to them.

JOHN DARLINGTON

CIVIL AND   MILITARY TAILOR,

AND

GENERAL OUTFITTER,

No. 5, BUADE STREET, U. T.,

QUEBEC.

SAMUEL WOODLEY,

Wholesale Boot and Shoe Manufacturer,

DIRECTS HIS WHOLE ATTENTION TO SEWED GOODS, AND SELLS TO THE WHOLESALE TRADE ONLY.

FACTORY, ST. JOACHIM STREET, ST. JOHN SUBURB,

QUEBEC.

S. Woodley's Retail Shoe Store and General Sewing Machine Depot. St. John Street.

QUEBEC BATH HOUSE,

HAIR DRESSING ROOM,

PALACE STREET, OPPOSITE RUSSELL'S HOTEL.

The Proprietor of the Quebec Bath House has neglected nothing to render his establishment as comfortable as can be desired.

5

NEWSPAPERS.

DUVERNAY, BROTHERS, Proprietors of *La Minerve*, Montreal, and of *Le Canada*, Ottawa, and General Agents for Collection of Claims against the Government of the Dominion of Canada and the Local Governments, York Street, Ottawa.

WATCHMAKERS.

C. S. SUTHERLAND,

Watch and Clock Maker,

RIDEAU STREET, OTTAWA,

WINE MERCHANTS.

K. ARNOLDI, Wine Merchant, No. 11, Metcalfe Street, Ottawa, confidently recommends and guarantees the following WINES, viz:—

No. 1 Port (good sound pr. gl. pr. doz.

			wine)	$2 00	$6 00
"	2	do	do	3 00	8 75
"	3	do	old	3 50	10 00
"	4	do	superior old	4 50	12 50
"	5	do	very fine old	5 75	15 50
"	1	Sherry, light table		2 00	6 00
"	2	"	superior do..	3 00	8 75
"	3	"	very choice..	3 50	10 00
"	4	"	choice old...	4 50	12 50
"	5	"	very fine.....	5 50	15 00
Marsala..............				1 30	4 00

Spirits, &c., of various brands—Purity of all Goods guaranteed. Price Lists, &c., on application. Orders by mail with cash or city reference promptly attended to. No charge for delivery in the city. A discount made to persons buying in quantity or original packages. Inspection respectfully solicited. K. ARNOLDI, Wine and Spirit Merchant, Metcalfe Street, Telegraph Co.'s Building, Ottawa.
October 17, 1867.

DRUGGISTS.

W. HEARN, Market Drug Store, York Street, Ottawa, Dealer in Spectacles, Microscopes, Thermometers, Barometers and all kinds of Optical Instruments and Philosophical Apparatus. Photographic Chemicals always on hand.

LEATHER AND WAX WORKS.

MRS. J. CLIFFORD teaches the following branches of art: German Leather Work, Flowers, Fruits and Statuettes in wax, Oriental painting and other fancy works of art. Charges moderate. St. George Street, Ottawa.

GROCERS.

M. SPARROW & CO., Importers and Dealers in Groceries, Liquors and Provisions, Wholesale and Retail, Sparrow's Building, corner of Sussex and Murray Streets, Ottawa.

HOTELS.

CHAMPAGNE'S HOTEL.—I. Champagne begs to inform his numerous patrons that he has again resumed business in the city, opposite *Le Canada* Office, York Street, charges moderate.
N. B.—Stabling for seven span of horses and good yard attached.

HOTEL DU CANADA.

B. B. LARIVIÈRE begs to call the attention of his friends from the Province of Quebec and elsewhere, that he has opened TWO HOTELS, one in Sparrow's Block, corner of Sussex and Murray Streets, and the other in the Bishop's large Brick House, Sussex Street. Both these Hotels are situated in the best part of the City, quite near the Government Buildings, and at a few paces to the Railway Station and Steamboat Wharf. The rooms are large, well ventilated, and furnished in the latest style. His constant attention will be devoted to the comfort of travellers. Omnibus in attendance for the arrivals and departures of Railway and Steamboat. Ottawa, 22nd October, 1867.

BOWLING SALOON.

OTTAWA BOWLING SALOON, corner of Murray and Sussex Streets. W. A. Cameron, proprietor. Best kinds of Liquors always on hand. Dancing Rooms opened twice a week.

BAGS.

FOR SALE AT LOW PRICES, Grain Flour, and other Bags, now on hand and arriving, a large assortment of various qualities, at LAING & COUPAR'S, 377, *Commissioners Street, Montreal.*

MUSIC STORES.

LONDON MUSIC STORE, Sign of the Big Fiddle, opposite the Russell House, where will be found one of the largest and best collection of Piano Fortes, from the Union Co., Steinway and Gahler;—and also all sorts of Musical Instruments. Pianos & Accordeons tuned. Quadrille Bands for Evening parties.   **E. MILES.**
Ottawa, Nov. 1867.

TAILORS.

T. RAJOTTE Begs leave to announce that he has commenced business as manufacturer of **Clothing of every description**, IMPORTER of CLOTHS, TWEEDS, &c. WHOLESALE and RETAIL, and that he has secured the services of a first class cutter, and an experienced staff of workmen. An early inspection of stock is solicited.
No. 32, SPARKS St., OTTAWA.

Dr. JOHN LEGGO,

DENTIST,

HUNTON'S BLOCK,

No. 49, Sparks Street,

CENTRAL OTTAWA.

THE MEDICAL HALL.

CHARLES AUSTIN,

Pharmaceutical Chemist & Druggist,

41, RIDEAU STREET, OTTAWA.

Importer and Dealer in Drugs and Chemicals, Druggists' Sundries, Dye Stuffs, &c., &c.

PRESCRIPTIONS AND FAMILY RECEIPTS CAREFULLY PREPARED.

J. P. M. LECOURT,

ARCHITECT AND CIVIL ENGINEER.

Residence : Old Grey Sisters Convent, North side St. Patrick street, between Sussex and Dalhousie streets, (Near the Bishop's Palace,)

OTTAWA.

DR. WOOD,

SPARKS STREET and MARIA STREET,

Ottawa, C. W.

CANCERS CURED

By a new, but certain, speedy, and nearly painless process, and without
the use of the knife. The cure will be guaranteed, and, as a
proof of this, no pay is required, until the cure is complete.
The moment a cancer is discovered, it should be cured
as it will cost less and is more speedily cured than
when of longer standing, and there is nothing
to gain, and everything to lose by delay.
What now seems a harmless lump in
the breast, neck, eye-lid or elsewhere, or small wart or sore on
the lip, may, in a few short months,
become a hideous, disgusting, destroying mass of
disease. If required, references can be given to parties
who have been cured many years since, and who are now sound
and healthy.

ALL COMMUNICATIONS PROMPTLY ANSWERED.

DEPARTMENT OF THE SECRETARY OF STATE OF CANADA.

OTTAWA, 23rd October, 1867.

PUBLIC NOTICE is hereby given that all Communications relating to Indian Affairs and Lands, or to the affairs of Ordnance Lands belonging to Canada, are in future to be addressed to " *The Honorable the Secretary of State for Canada, Ottawa.*"

ETIENNE PARENT,
Under Secretary of State for Canada.

GEO. FUTVOYE, Q. C.,

FOR LOWER CANADA,

NOTARY PUBLIC FOR UPPER CANADA.

And Commissioner for taking Affidavits to be received in any of the Courts of

LOWER CANADA, AND UPPER CANADA,

Or in those sitting at

WESTMINSTER.

349, WELLINGTON STREET,

OTTAWA.

SALMON RIVERS.

DEPARTMENT OF MARINE AND FISHERIES,

Ottawa, 7th October, 1867.

LIST of SALMON RIVERS within the Province of Quebec, the Fluvial Divisions of which are disposable for Angling purposes :—

The River Mistassimi—discharging into River St. Lawrence on the North Shore.

"	Betscie	"	"	"	"
"	Trinity	"	"	"	"
"	Little Trinity	"	"	"	"
"	Calumet	"	"	"	"
"	Pentecost	"	"	"	"
"	Little Margaret	"	"	"	"
"	Trout	"	"	"	"
"	Sheldrake	"	"	"	"
"	Magpie	"	"	"	"
"	Little Watscheeshoo	"	"	"	"
"	Nabesippi	"	"	"	"
"	Agwanus	"	"	"	"
"	Kegashka	"	"	"	"
"	Musquarro	"	"	"	"
"	Washeecootai	"	"	"	"
"	Romaine (en bas)	"	"	"	"
"	Coacoacho	"	"	"	"
"	Etamarru	"	"	"	"
"	Macatima	"	"	"	"
"	St. Augustine	"	"	"	"
"	Esquimaux	"	"	"	"
"	Ouelle	"	"	"	South Shore.
"	Metis	"	"	"	"
"	Ste. Anne des Monts	"	"	"	"
"	Mont Louis	"	"	"	"
"	Magdalen	"	"	"	"
"	Grand Pabos	"	Chaleur Bay	"	"
"	" Bonaventure	"	"	"	"
"	Little Cascapedia	"	"	"	"
"	Grand Cascapedia	"	"	"	"
"	Nouvelle	"	"	"	"
"	Matapedia	"	"	"	"
"	Restigouche	"	"	"	"
"	Mistouche	"	"	"	"

Application to lease or license any of the above Rivers should be made to this Department.

P. MITCHELL,
Minister of Marine and Fisheries.